PHOTOGRAPHS BY MELBA LEVICK

TEXT BY GINA HYAMS

in a Mexican Garden

courtyards, pools, and open-air living rooms

CHRONICLE BOOKS

SAN FRANCISCO

Page 176 constitutes a continuation of the copyright page.

Library of Congress Cataloging-in-Publication Data available.

ISBN 0-8118-4130-8

Manufactured in China.

Designed by Alan Smithee
Typeset by Deborah Bowman

Distributed in Canada by
Raincoast Books
9050 Shaughnessy Street
Vancouver, British Columbia V6P 6E5

10 9 8 7 6 5 4 3 2 1

Chronicle Books LLC
85 Second Street
San Francisco, California 94105

www.chroniclebooks.com

DEDICATION

To my mother and father, whose love and generosity have sustained and inspired me.

M.L.

For my husband, Dave, with whom I am always found, no matter how lost.

G.H.

PAGE 2: Exuberant potted impatiens and geraniums crowd the fountain at Casa Correo in San Miguel de Allende. Locally crafted brass frogs, turtles, and lizards parade around the ledge.

TABLE OF CONTENTS

INTRODUCTION

"Flowers rain down, they interweave, whirl about,
they come to bring joy upon the earth."

—Cacamatzin, sixteenth-century Aztec poet

In a Mexican Garden is about the joy of outdoor living. In Mexico, gardens are designed to be lived in rather than to impress the neighbors. Cloistered behind high walls, they are private oases, perfect for reflection or afternoon siestas, as well as the places where family and friends gather to feast and celebrate. Plant-filled courtyards are humanizing slices of nature in the midst of urban commotion; they offer cool refuge from the mid-day heat. In these secluded rooms without roofs, various elements mingle—indoors and out, sunshine and moonlight, the quiet babble of fountains and the exuberant cries of mariachi bands. ❁ Since ancient times, the people of Mexico have delighted in the natural world and drawn spiritual inspiration from it. Nature was at the center of the pre-Columbian cosmology. The early people worshipped the sun, moon, and rain as gods. For them, oceans and mountain springs were magic, and wind symbolized the creative spirit, the breath from which life derived. The Aztecs so revered nature that they worshipped three distinct flower gods—Xochipilli, Macuilxochitl, and Xochiquetzal—who served as the patrons of beauty, pleasure, and the arts. ❁ The notion of cultivated gardens in Mexico stretches back to the Mixtec creation myth (circa A.D. 750–1500) in which two young boy deities named Wind of Nine Snakes and Wind of the Caves planted a garden of sweet-smelling fruit trees, flowering shrubs, and herbs as a pious offering to their parents in order to bring light to the world. To strengthen their prayers, the boys

OPPOSITE: Forty-million-year-old geodes make a statement on this hard-edged unpolished marble table at Casa la Roca in Pátzcuaro. The patio plant containers are equally massive in scale, bursting with ferns, phormium, and a sago palm. The decorative finial, called a *pirindongo*, is a contemporary ceramic version of the Spanish Colonial stone ornament.

TOP: This striking contemporary fountain made of copper, stone, tile, and cement graces the lawn at Casa Fresno Grande in San Miguel de Allende; it complements the clean symmetry of the mauve pavillion behind.

ABOVE: An iguana sips from a spiral granite fountain designed by Eduardo Olbés at Casa del Alacran in Tepoztlán.

OPPOSITE, TOP: Shiny emerald-green pots from the state of Mexico adorn the loggia at Casa la Roca in Pátzcuaro. The stone balls are natural geodes; the yellow lion is a Mexican carousel figure from the early twentieth century.

pierced their tongues and ears with sharp knives made of flint, and sprinkled the blood on the plants with a brush made of willow twigs. Their prayers were answered, and thus life on earth began. ❁ From that first mythic garden on, a passion for gardens flourished throughout the pre-Columbian world. When the Spanish conquerors invaded the New World in A.D. 1519, they were astonished by the sophistication of the Aztec city of Tenochtitlán, with its massive temple pyramids adorned with magnificent frescoes and intricately carved stone panels, mosaics, and statuary. They were also dazzled by the water canals, public parks, botanical garden, and zoo. In his eye-witness account, *The Conquest of New Spain,* conquistador Bernal Díaz del Castillo described the city as seeming "like an enchanted vision . . . [and that] some of the soldiers asked whether it was not all a dream." ❁ The Spaniards were especially impressed with the Aztec ruler Montezuma's personal garden. Montezuma's estate was so enormous it was said to require a staff of 300 gardeners. His miles and miles of terraced flower beds were ablaze with dahlias, marigolds, poinsettias, and frangipani. Freshwater and saltwater ponds, cascading fountains, meandering pathways, and shade pavilions were scattered throughout the grounds. The palace itself was designed for outdoor living, structured around patios and open arcades. ❁ The Spanish also had a venerable history of architecture that encompassed the pleasures of outdoor living. The famous Alhambra garden, with its ornate plantings, myriad fountains, and bubbling pools, dates from the thirteenth century. The Moorish tradition of courtyards adapted well to the New World's temperate climate. Spanish Colonial homes typically included at least one interior patio graced with a carved stone fountain. Surrounding the patio, arches or columns supported a roofed corridor that opened into the rooms of the house. These open-air living spaces provided shade, air circulation, and protection from wind and rain. Houses that the Spanish built more than 400 years ago in Mexico remain well preserved, and the classic style continues to be emulated in new buildings. ❁ Contemporary Mexican architecture is characterized by a minimalist aesthetic. The sculptural use of cement is often combined with a palette of blood reds, sun-drenched pinks, deep ochers, and radiant blues. These buildings tend to have a stark geometric quality, but like their pre-Columbian and Spanish Colonial predecessors, are tranquil, welcoming spaces that incorporate nature into their design. Pioneering modern Mexican architect Luis Barragán (1902–1988) explained: "In my gardens, in my homes, I have always tried to make the placid murmur of silence prevail." ❁ Mexico is home to more than 25,000 species of plants, making it one of the richest horticultural regions on earth. The diversity of plant life ranges from desert cacti to dense pine forests to tropical palms swaying along the coast. Every region is full of avid gardeners. Even the most humble homes are made joyous with geraniums planted in tin cans. ❁ Mexican builders and artisans let their imaginations run free in patios and gardens. They craft charming statuary and garden ornaments and transform the most functional objects into items of beauty. Pathways become mosaic masterpieces. Swimming pools and stairways are occasions to decorate with hand-painted Talevera tile, and fountains are big vases to be filled with a thousand calla lilies. Walls are works of art in themselves or become vertical gardens covered with orchids, flame vines, and bougainvillea. ❁ The architectural focus created by courtyard walls somehow inspires a heightened sensual awareness. Gabriel García Márquez evokes the mystery and romance of this phenomenon in his novel *The General in His Labyrinth:* ". . . the scent of jasmine rose from the illuminated patio, the air seemed like diamonds, and there were more stars than ever in the sky." ❁ Indeed, photographer Melba Levick and I encountered many such courtyards in the course of creating this book. The project gave us a glorious excuse to knock on strangers' doors. We were greeted with nothing but generosity and kindness, and we are deeply indebted to all who received us with such warm hospitality. As we walked into each secret garden, we had the feeling that we were entering into a profoundly personal world. Full of whimsy and handcrafted splendor, each location embodied the idiosyncratic, heartfelt vision of its inhabitants, layered on top of contributions from generations of previous owners, builders, and artisans. The result is a vibrant historical fugue. ❁ Whether you use this book as a design resource, a travel guide, or simply as inspiration for daydreams of Mexico, we invite you to slow down and savor the wondrous colors and textures, and to breathe in the perfume of the flowers. In the words of Ayocuan, a sixteenth-century Aztec poet: "Let us be joyful, friends, there is welcome here. In this flowering land we live, where no one can destroy the flowers and the songs. They will endure in the house of the Giver of Life."

—G.H.

ABOVE: A diamond pattern of terra-cotta tiles and gray pebbles paves the pool terrace at Villa Montaña, where swimmers enjoy a panoramic view of the city of Morelia.

FOLLOWING PAGES: A row of antique earthenware molasses pots planted with spiky Sansevieria (sometimes known as "mother-in-law's tongue") decorates this patio wall at Casa de la Torre in Cuernavaca. The border of Japanese grass in front of the creeping fig creates a striking fringe effect.

The South

To have watched from one of your patios
the ancient stars,
from the bench of shadow to have watched
those scattered lights
that my ignorance has learned no names for
nor their places in constellations,
to have heard the note of water
in the cistern,
known the scent of jasmine and honeysuckle,
the silence of the sleeping bird,
the arch of the entrance, the damp
these things perhaps are the poem.

—Jorge Luis Borges

chapter

1

COURTYARDS

LEFT: Hotel Camino Real Oaxaca occupies the former premises of the sixteenth-century Santa Catalina Convent. The building's original decorative glory has been carefully restored, including the fresco paintings seen here above the courtyard arches. Bougainvillea vines cascade over the roof, spilling magenta blossoms on the cloistered garden below.

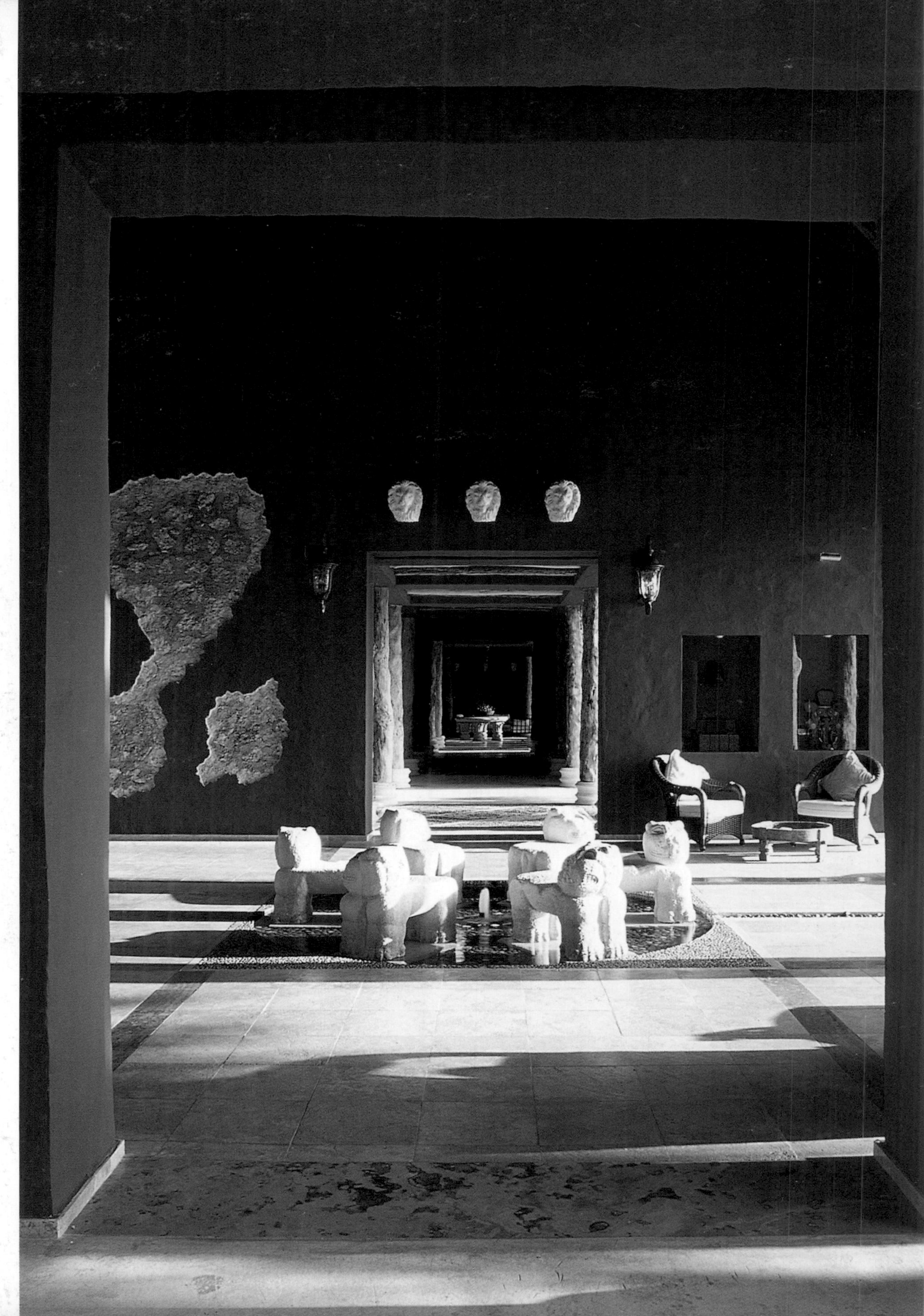

OPPOSITE: The architecture and décor of Paraiso de la Bonita Resort reflect both the indigenous Mayan culture and Spanish Colonial heritage of the Yucatán Peninsula. Soaring archways lead to a series of courtyards. A fountain made of six carved stone jaguar figures welcomes guests to the main house. The ancient Mayan people revered jaguars as deities associated with the power of warriors and the sun.

RIGHT: The front door opens directly from the street into a verdant interior courtyard at Casa Areca in San Miguel de Allende. A potted crimson cyclamen rests on a grinding stone table.

OPPOSITE: Hotel Casa Oaxaca serves as a rotating showcase for modern artists in Oaxaca City. Architect Jorge Quintanar Castillo refurbished the 200-year-old house by combining Spanish Colonial scale and traditional materials with a distinctly contemporary minimalist sensibility. Palm, pomegranate, and *zapote* trees ring a green *cantera* stone fountain in the courtyard. The beautiful ceramic pots make ideal containers for ferns.

LEFT: Throughout Hotel Casa Oaxaca, deep green ceramic pots from the nearby village of Santa Maria Atzompa serve as planters; this one is filled with white bougainvillea.

BELOW: These straight-backed wicker chairs were custom-designed for Hotel Casa Oaxaca by local interior designer Mercede Audelo. In the background, the bouquets of marigolds and votive candles are part of a *Dia de los Muertos* (Day of the Dead) altar.

In a Mexican Garden

LEFT: A constellation of frosted-glass stars illuminates an evening sky-blue patio wall at Casa Beso de las Estrellas (Kiss of the Stars House) in San Miguel de Allende. The floor is a swirling mosaic of russet and ocher-colored river stones and gray slate. The steel patio furniture was a Guadalajara flea market find. The chairs, originally outfitted with rattan seats, were refurbished with metal to make them suitable for outdoor use.

ABOVE: The architects of Casa Beso de las Estrellas, Cathi and Steven House, bathed their modern structure in a palette of mango, grape, and sage inspired by Mexican architect Luis Barragán's bold juxtaposition of colors. Natural mineral paint pigments give the walls their translucent, luminous glow.

ABOVE: La Casa Encantada (The Enchanted House) is an eighteenth-century Spanish Colonial mansion in Pátzcuaro that now functions as an artists' retreat center. A star-shaped Christmas piñata decorates the courtyard.

RIGHT: The courtyard at La Casa Encantada, with its warm terra-cotta tiles and lush plantings, is an inviting spot in which to court creative inspiration.

OPPOSITE AND ABOVE: At Casa Luna Quebrada in San Miguel de Allende, owner Dianne Kushner takes advantage of the roof overhang to display big ceramic pots planted with bougainvilleas.

OPPOSITE, TOP, AND RIGHT: Virginia creeper vines climb the wall and fall over this row of ceramic pots at Casa Luna Quebrada; philodendron frames the courtyard arch.

OPPOSITE, BOTTOM: A jumble of earthenware pots and recycled tin can planters make for a charming entry garden on the steps at Casa Luna Pila Seca in San Miguel de Allende. Cracked or chipped pottery gets a second life when used as outdoor decoration.

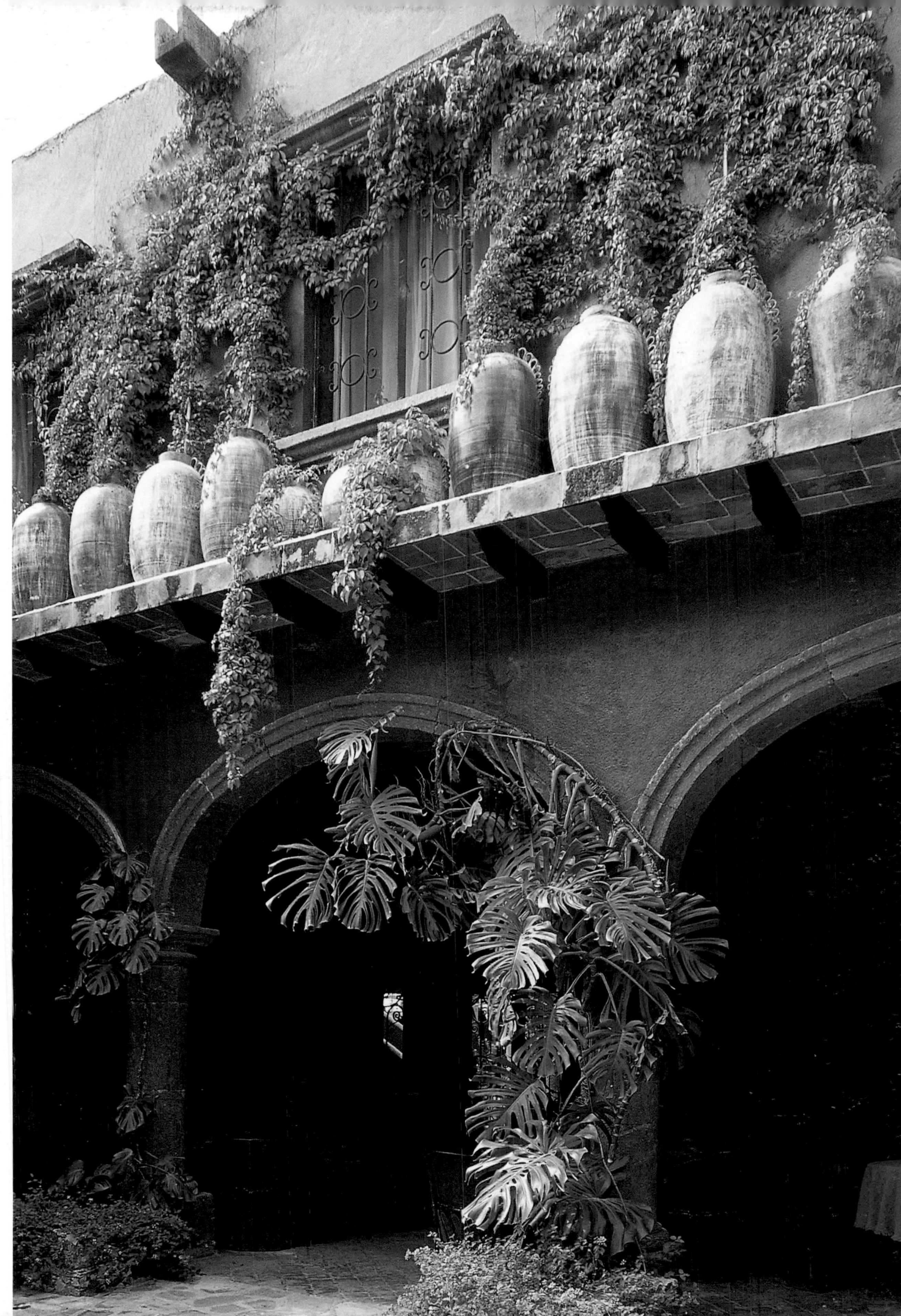

BELOW: The loggias of La Casa de la Cuesta (The House of the Hill) in San Miguel de Allende serve double duty as living spaces and art galleries. Homeowners Heidi and Bill Levasseur's Mexican folk art collection includes more than 400 masks that were originally used in indigenous religious dance ceremonies.

RIGHT: This tabletop display includes boxes and crosses encrusted with *milagros* (silver charms that are traditionally used to petition for miracles), Posada-inspired *calaca* (skeleton) figures, and a Oaxacan ceramic bowl ringed with embracing lovers. On the floor sits a blue vase from nearby Dolores Hidalgo and a large wooden mortar and pestle. The ceremonial masks on the wall come from the states of Puebla, Veracruz, and Hidalgo; each is more than fifty years old.

OPPOSITE: Spanish Colonial–style mahogany furnishings mix easily with the rustic green hutch and *equipal* coffee table. The three contemporary *papel amate* (handmade paper) pieces hung on the wall are from the Otomí village of San Pablito in Puebla. The papermaking technique dates back hundreds of years to the pre-Columbian era. Artisans boil and soak *jonote* tree (ficus family) bark in a mixture of water, ashes, and lime; they hammer the pulp with a small, flat stone, and then let the sheets of paper dry in the sun. To the right, Xantolo (beggar) masks from Day of the Dead festivities are creatively framed in a drawer from an antique desk.

chapter
2

SPANISH COLONIAL LOGGIAS

OPPOSITE, TOP: The second-floor loggia at La Casa de la Cuesta is a choice gathering spot to drink margaritas and watch the sunset. Sheltered from the elements, the space allows for the enjoyment of the outdoors no matter what the weather. As the traditional Mexican saying goes: "How beautiful to watch the rain and not get wet."

OPPOSITE, BOTTOM LEFT: The *equipal* dining table is made festive with a rainbow-striped mat. The *papel amate* (handmade paper) piece on the wall depicts the Otomí god of oranges.

OPPOSITE, BOTTOM RIGHT: An old sugarcane press becomes a showcase for glazed green and blue pineapple-shaped jars from the village of San José de Gracia in Michoacán.

RIGHT: A corner fireplace, graced by a hand-painted tile mural of the Virgin of Guadalupe, heats the open-air living space. The two-piece horse figures on either side of the fireplace are from the state of Guerrero. The horses' heads and tails are held up with suspenders and worn during the Dance of the Santiagueros, a ceremony dating back to the Spanish Conquest that celebrates the battles between the Christians and infidels.

FAR LEFT: Ornate wrought-iron gates open to the tranquil loggia seating areas of Casa Luna Quebrada in San Miguel de Allende.

CENTER: Oversized *equipal* chairs, made of hardwood splits and pigskin lashed together with maguey fiber, are proportionally in balance with the high ceilings and expansive feeling of this indoor-outdoor space. The indigo-colored cushions are made of hand-loomed Guatemalan fabric. The Moorish-style quatrefoil window is known as an *ojo de buey* (oxen eye).

LEFT: This copper lighting fixture, based on a Moroccan design, was custom-made for Casa Luna Quebrada in San Miguel de Allende.

ABOVE: A low wall, painted an unexpected shade of aqua, separates the loggia from the courtyard garden at Casa Brunson Bed and Breakfast in Pátzcuaro. The garden, a delightful blend of formal and casual elements, is abloom.

OPPOSITE: Two huge ceramic candelabras fit perfectly into the *cantera* stone niche. The decorative shells are carved in a classic Spanish Colonial motif.

LEFT: This intriguing stone object is a nineteenth-century Mexican water filter. The wooden pitchfork remains from the days when horses were kept at the back of the house and hens and roosters ran free on the kitchen patio.

RIGHT: This charming set of wooden spoons, forks, and *molinillos* (hot chocolate whisks) was carved in the nearby village of Cuanajo; it adorns the loggia just outside the kitchen. On the floor are two *molcajetes* (mortars) made of rough volcanic rock. These are used for grinding chilies, garlic, and other herbs and spices.

FAR RIGHT: Pátzcuaro's La Casa de la Real Aduana (House of the Royal Customs) was built in 1537. The copper funnel captures water from a rainspout off the roof.

LEFT: Mexico's haciendas were large plantations and cattle ranches. Thanks to the henequen (sisal) boom years of 1880 to 1920, the Yucatán Peninsula is especially rich with grand estates. Within a 75-mile radius of the capital city of Mérida, there are said to be more than 400 haciendas. Some of these properties are in ruin, but in recent years, many have been restored and converted into private homes and deluxe resorts.

Each hacienda contained a *casa principal* (main house) where the owner lived and where business was conducted. Framed by a series of graceful arches, the *casa principal* at Hacienda Santa Rosa is now a hotel lobby and restaurant.

BELOW AND OPPOSITE: The robin's egg–blue facade, stenciled ocher walls, and brick-red tile floor have been restored to look just as they did when the hacienda was built in the early twentieth century.

chapter

3

HACIENDA LOGGIAS

ABOVE: Villa Santa Anna in Mérida is a former home of Antonio López de Santa Anna (1794–1876), who served an astounding eleven terms as Mexico's president. The mansion flows around three atmospheric courtyards. These archways are romantically cloaked with butterfly pea vine. Other creative plantings serve to soften the effect of symmetry and hard surfaces.

OPPOSITE: A Moorish quatrefoil-shaped fountain ringed with Manila palms forms the centerpiece of the front courtyard.

BELOW: Dramatic red tones and elegant black-and-white striped pillars set the stage at the rear loggia of Villa Santa Anna.

OPPOSITE, TOP: The French-inspired white wrought-iron patio chairs hearken back to President Porfirio Díaz's era (roughly 1876–1911), when Mexican aristocrats were enamored with all things European.

OPPOSITE, BOTTOM: The rear loggia faces a lush garden. The natural setting is carried onto the porch with a delicate vine stencil pattern along the back wall. Pots of marigolds mixed with agave provide a stunning contrast to the border of wild ginger plants.

OPPOSITE: A Spanish Colonial landmark, Hacienda Chichén Resort is located just outside the grounds of the famous tenth-century Mayan ruin Chichén Itzá. The front terrace floor is paved with hand-carved stone, matching the *cantera* columns. Rough-hewn wood roof beams add to the rustic charm, and the potted plants tie the space to the tropical jungle just beyond the front steps.

ABOVE: The breakfast table is set with a cobalt-blue tablecloth, festive ribbons, and decorative tins filled with almonds. A typical morning meal includes orange and watermelon juices and *rosca brioche* (almond and cream cheese sweet bread) slathered in the hacienda's own wildflower honey—all to be savored while admiring the beautifully maintained formal gardens.

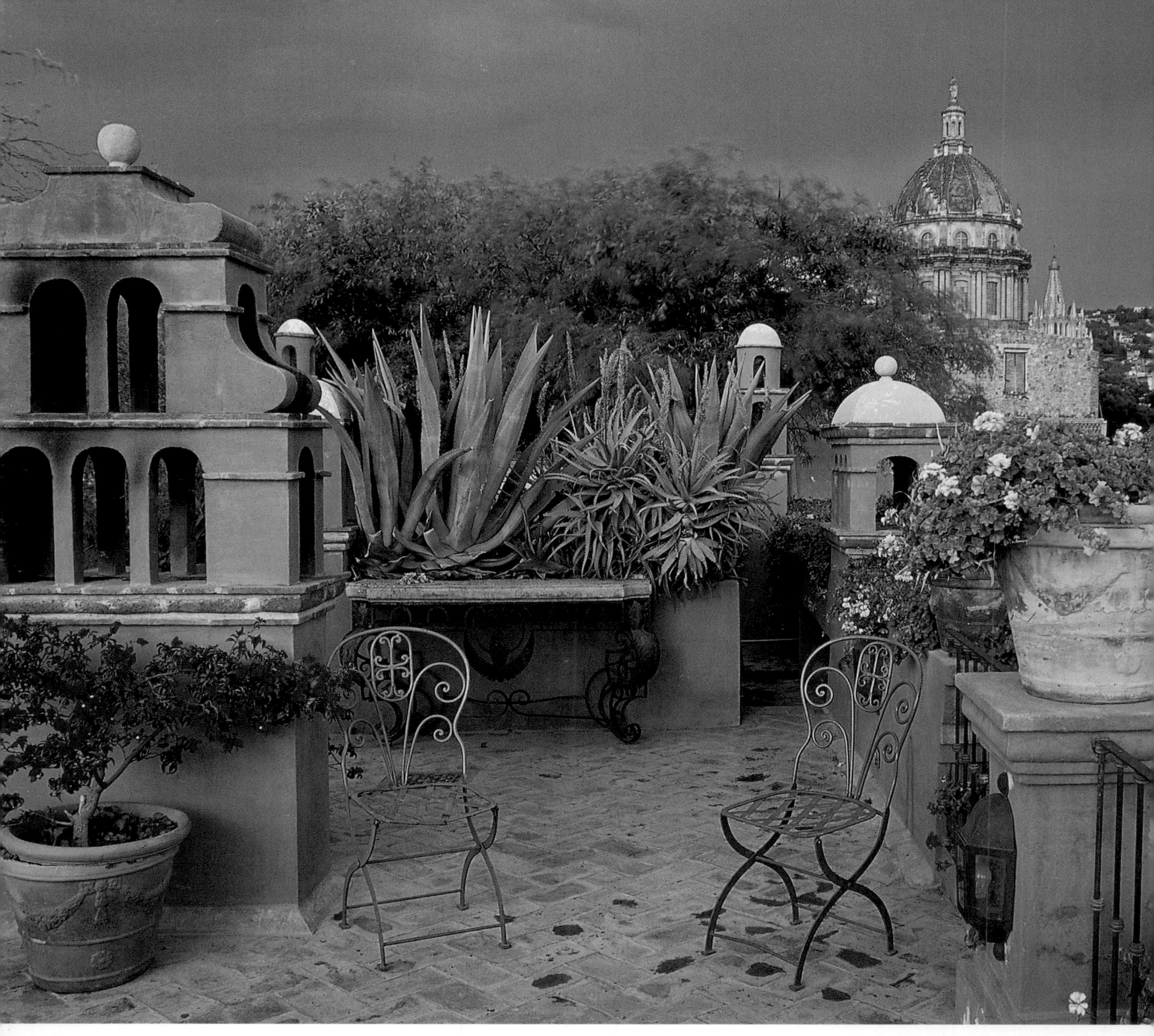

ABOVE: Agave and aloe vera thrive in a built-in planter on the roof at Quinta Quebrada in San Miguel de Allende.

OPPOSITE: The Quinta Quebrada upper terrace garden is a fiesta of color—a classic Mexican combination of magenta bougainvillea, red geraniums, and violet-blue jacaranda tree blossoms.

chapter
4

ROOFTOP TERRACES

ABOVE: In the morning light, the pink-tipped fountain grass appears lit from within on the rooftop terrace at Casa Areca in San Miguel de Allende. Purple and yellow bougainvillea and the exotic leaves of a papaya complete the tropical oasis.

OPPOSITE: The balustrade is decorated with a mix of pink and red geraniums planted in terra-cotta pots. The winch is used to transport supplies from the ground level two stories below.

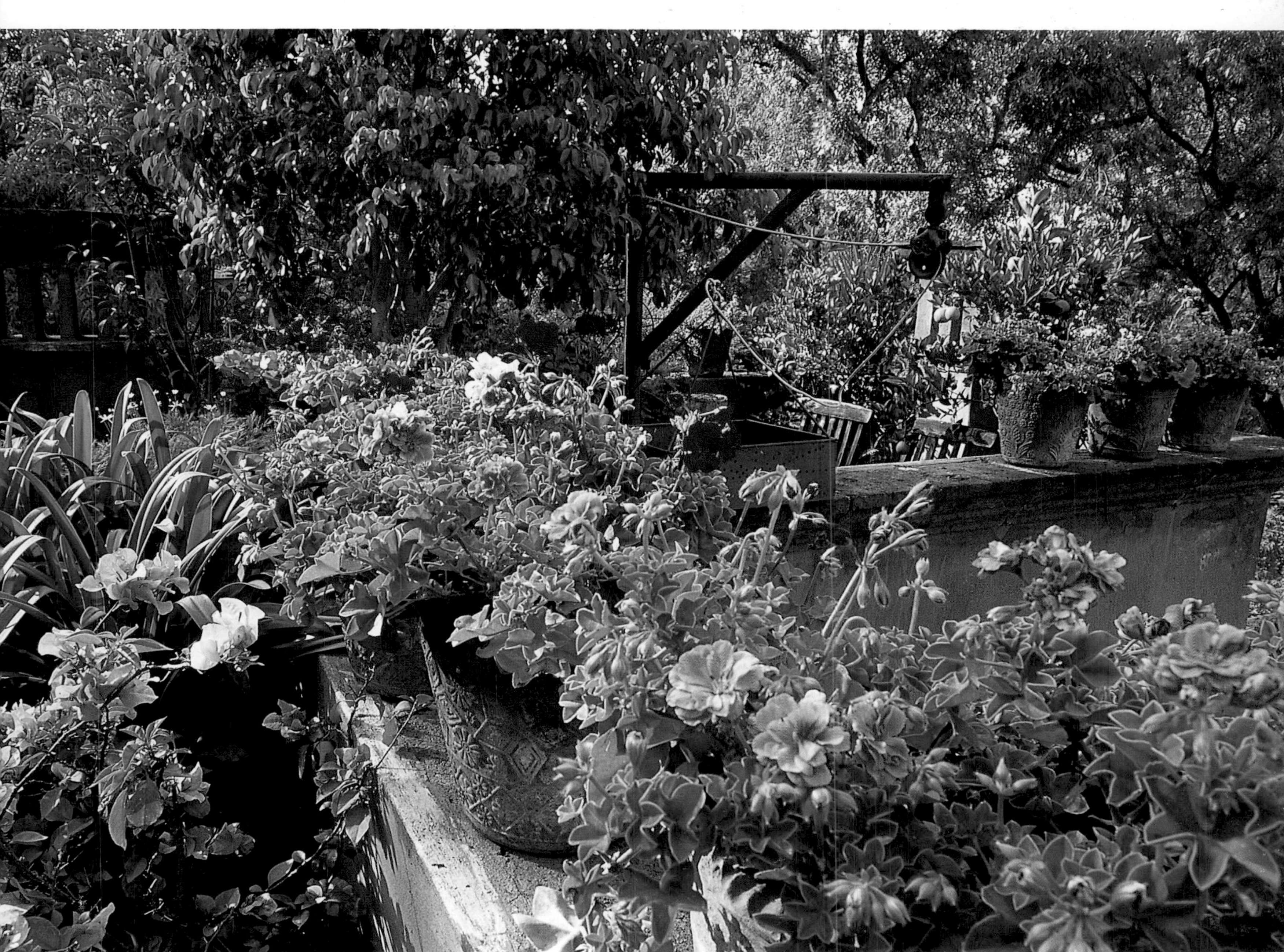

OPPOSITE: At Casa Correo in San Miguel de Allende, the dining table centerpiece, a miniature ceramic church, mirrors the church seen in the distance, El Oratorio de San Felipe Neri.

ABOVE: A bedspread emblazoned with the Virgin of Guadalupe blesses a chaise longue at Casa Sierra Negra del Sur (Black Mountain South House) in San Miguel de Allende. Rose-shaped pillows designed by expatriate artist Susan Plum soften the built-in concrete bench. Orange flame vines crawl up the rag-washed blue wall and over the painted-green iron pergola.

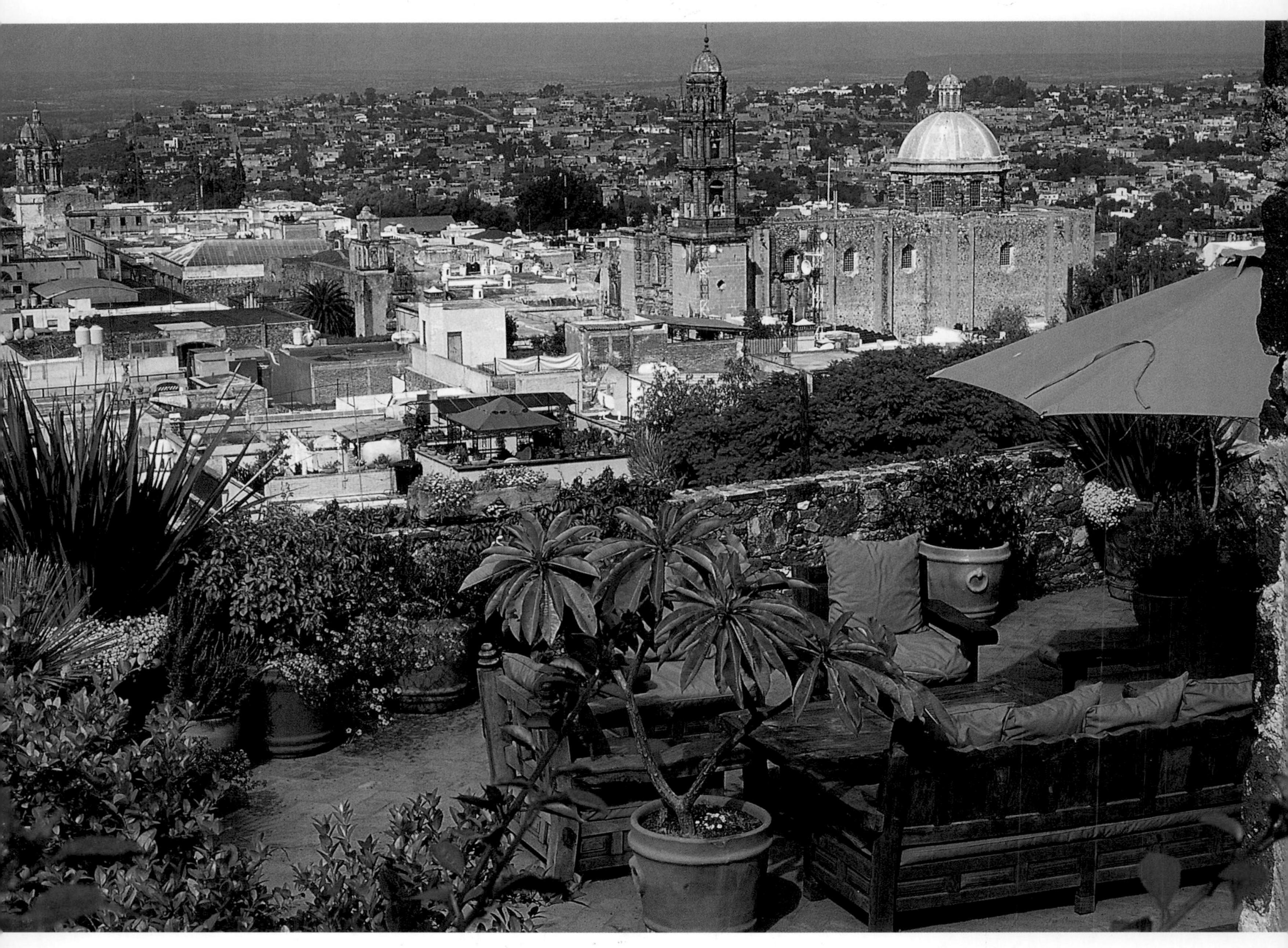

ABOVE: The rooftop terrace of Casa Chupa Rosa (Hummingbird House) affords a panoramic view of San Miguel de Allende. Among the potted plants near the terrace sitting area are fragrant frangipani, lavender, and rosemary.

OPPOSITE, TOP: A pergola trellis covered with flowering blue trumpet vines provides shade on the roof at Casa de Los Cinco Perros (House of the Five Dogs) in San Miguel de Allende.

OPPOSITE, BOTTOM: An impressively gnarled old mesquite tree, some two stories tall, grows in the central courtyard at Casa Seis Fuentes (Six Fountains House) in San Miguel de Allende.

BELOW: Twisting mahogany tree trunks support the Palapa Beach Club's thatched roof at Las Alamandas on the Pacific Coast. Bright yellow throw pillows accent the built-in cement couch.

OPPOSITE: Shaggy thatched umbrellas shade beachside tables at Dos Ceibas in Tulum.

chapter
5

PALAPAS

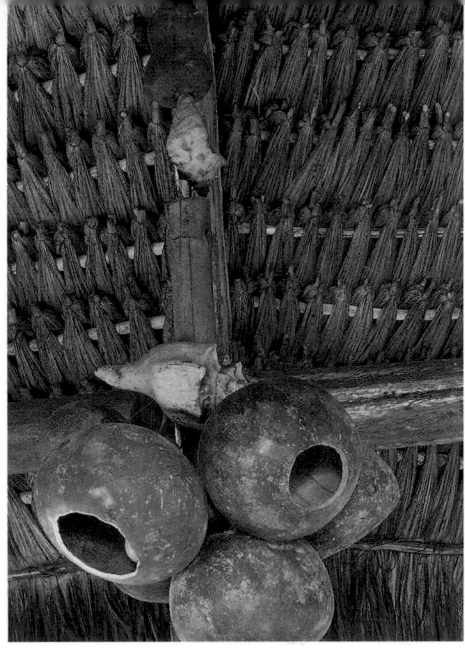

LEFT: Conch shells and gourds decorate this *palapa* roof at Maroma Resort. The rustic lighting fixture is made from coconuts.

BELOW: Built *poco a poco* over a period of fifteen years, Maroma Resort has evolved into one of the most luxurious hideaways on the Riviera Maya. Architect José Luis Moreno never used formal blueprints for the project; instead, he drew his free-flowing Moorish-Mayan buildings in the sand and then called on local masons to implement his designs.

ABOVE: Two handmade clay pots form the base of the dining table at Villa Capricornio. The room is adorned with art pieces and objects that have special meaning for the family, including a portrait of the Morenos by painter Bertrand Castelli and a decorated papier-mâché egg by popular Mexican artist Sergio Bustamante.

LEFT: Villa Capricornio (Capricorn Villa) is the private residence of Maroma Resort founder and architect José Luis Moreno and his wife, Sally Shaw Moreno. The traditional Yucatecan thatched roof is fashioned from native *xit* palm sustainably harvested from their seaside ranch. The ancient Mayans carried *xit* palm seeds with them for protection; the hard red seed represented a symbolic roof over their heads.

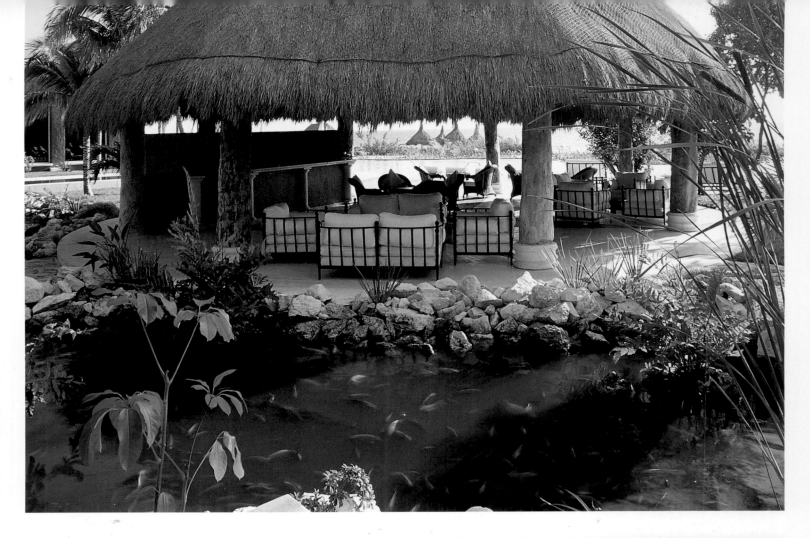

ABOVE: Paraiso de la Bonita Resort is located twelve miles south of Cancún on secluded Petenpich Bay. A rocky pond teeming with ornamental fish sits adjacent to the thatched-roof pool bar.

RIGHT: These cushy white couches have lightweight aluminum frames, which make them easy to reconfigure into various sitting arrangements. A pack of fierce Mayan jaguar figures faces the koi pond.

OPPOSITE: Owner and architect Carlos Gosselin has filled Paraiso de la Bonita Resort with treasures from his travels around the world. The lounge lighting fixture is constructed out of seventeenth-century monkey cages from the China-India border, and the palace-shaped birdcage hails from Indonesia. On the back wall, a painting of lemons and birds by Mexican artist Gerardo Zuñiga adds a whimsical touch.

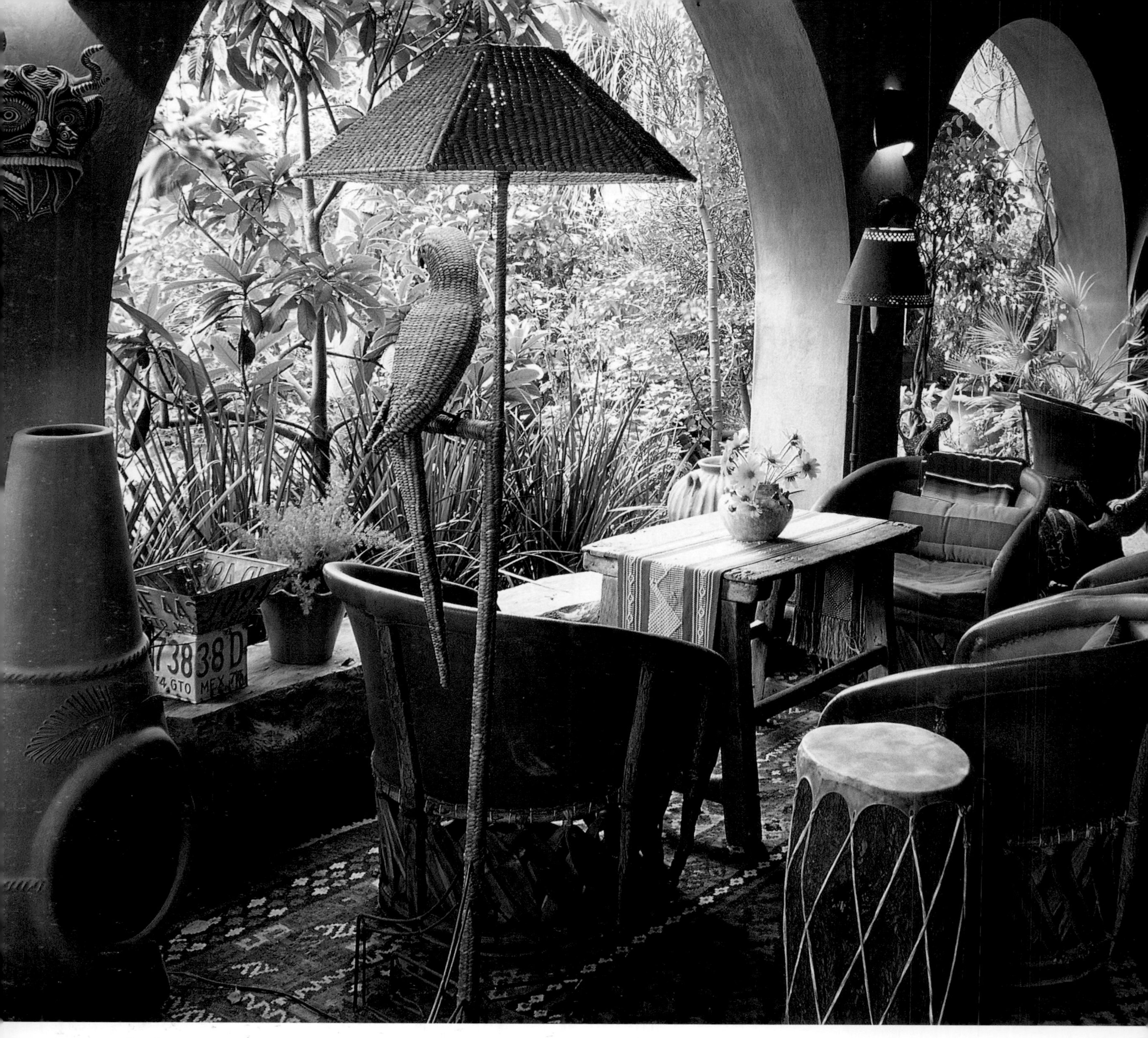

ABOVE: Pink and purple arches frame the view of the garden from the living room at Casa de Los Cinco Perros in San Miguel de Allende. A freestanding *chimenea* (ceramic fireplace) provides warmth on cool winter nights. The parrot lamp is a creation of artist Mario Lopez, who lives in Ihuatzio, a small village on the shores of Lake Pátzcuaro. The lamp is made from iron wrapped in tule; the parrot's eyes and beak are made from hand-beaten copper. The devil mask with two tongues is from Ocumicho, a town in Michoacán known for its surreal clay sculptures.

chapter

6

OPEN-AIR LIVING ROOMS

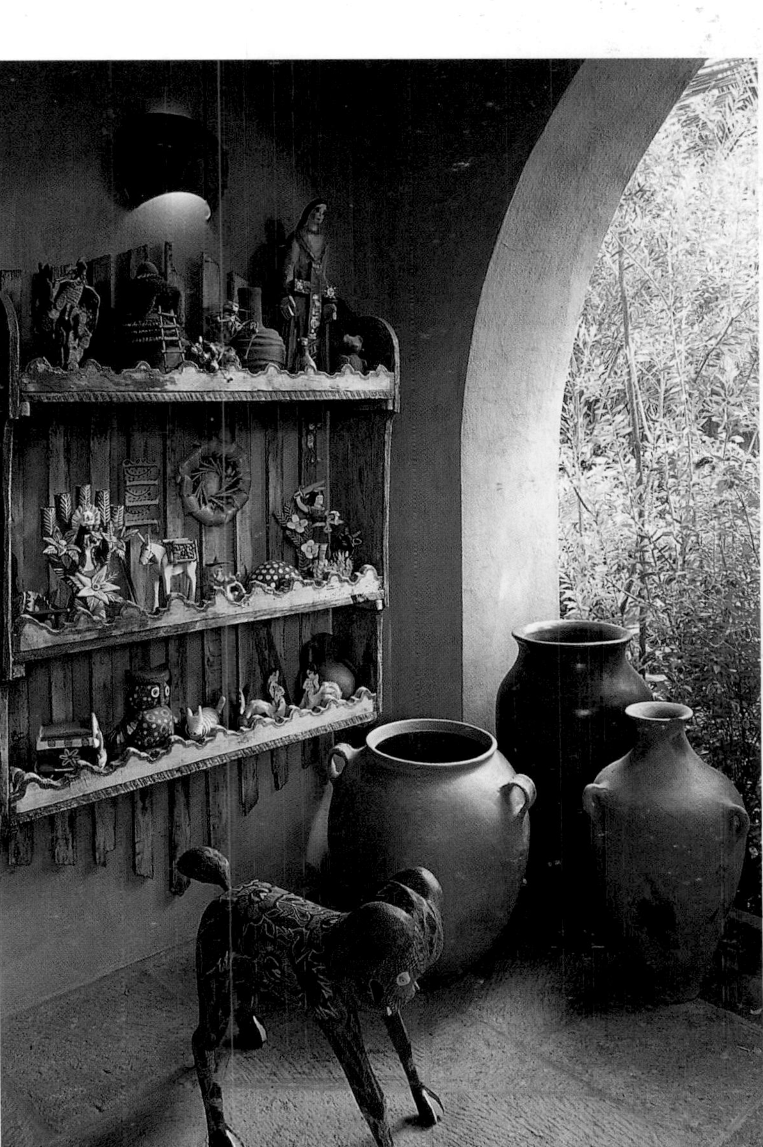

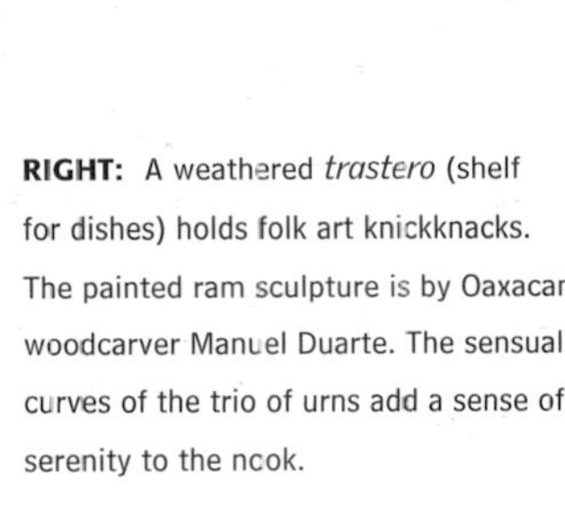

RIGHT: A weathered *trastero* (shelf for dishes) holds folk art knickknacks. The painted ram sculpture is by Oaxacan woodcarver Manuel Duarte. The sensual curves of the trio of urns add a sense of serenity to the nook.

ABOVE: Architects José Antonio Gonzalez and Miguel Angel Bustos and interior designer Roberto Laredo created a masterpiece in Casa El Deseo (The Desire House). Located in the village of Tehuixtla, near Cuernavaca, the house takes full advantage of the region's temperate climate with many indoor-outdoor living spaces.

RIGHT: A clay sculpture by Mexico City artist Javier Marín reclines adjacent to the elegant dining table.

OPPOSITE: The design team's modernist aesthetic complements the owner's contemporary art collection. Note how the square shape of Oaxacan artist Alvaro Santiago's painting echoes the shapes of the coffee table and the fireplace. The dramatic rectangular cutout next to the fireplace frames the trunks of mature trees.

OPPOSITE, TOP AND BOTTOM: At Quinta Quebrada in San Miguel de Allende, gilded religious artifacts and Spanish Colonial antiques mix with *equipal* furniture and contemporary Talavera pottery. The overall effect creates a harmonious blend of high and low, ornate and rustic. Window-sized mirrors reflect garden and sky, contributing to a sense of seamless flow between indoors and out.

BELOW: At Casa Seis Fuentes in San Miguel de Allende, symmetrical archways, potted pygmy date palms, and candlesticks situated on either side of the fireplace lend balance and grandeur to the open-air living room. The stately candlesticks are relics from a Catholic church. In the background, a spouting ram's head fountain pours into the tiled swimming pool. Three clay molds once used for making papier-mâché *puta* dolls sit on the coffee table. In the early twentieth century, the brightly painted dolls were placed in windows to advertise ladies of the night, but they have since lost this meaning and are now simply appreciated as charming Mexican folk art. The coconuts open up to form nut bowls.

ABOVE: The oldest wing of Casa Leof in Cuernavaca dates back to the sixteenth century, when it was built as part of a cathedral. Remodeled and expanded in the mid-1960s, the house maintains the epic scale of the original structure, with lofty ceilings and this enormous fireplace.

OPPOSITE, TOP: A rusty old iron cross adorns this weathered stone wall at Casa Chupa Rosa in San Miguel de Allende. Makeshift basket lampshades and pillows covered with bright Mexican blankets and woven straw mats make this open-air living room casual and inviting.

OPPOSITE, BOTTOM: The gazebo-like open-air living room at Quinta Los Almendros in Mérida has a contemporary flair with its glass-topped rattan tables and sleek chairs. The garden is equally stylish, planted in strokes of green, magenta, and pale yellow.

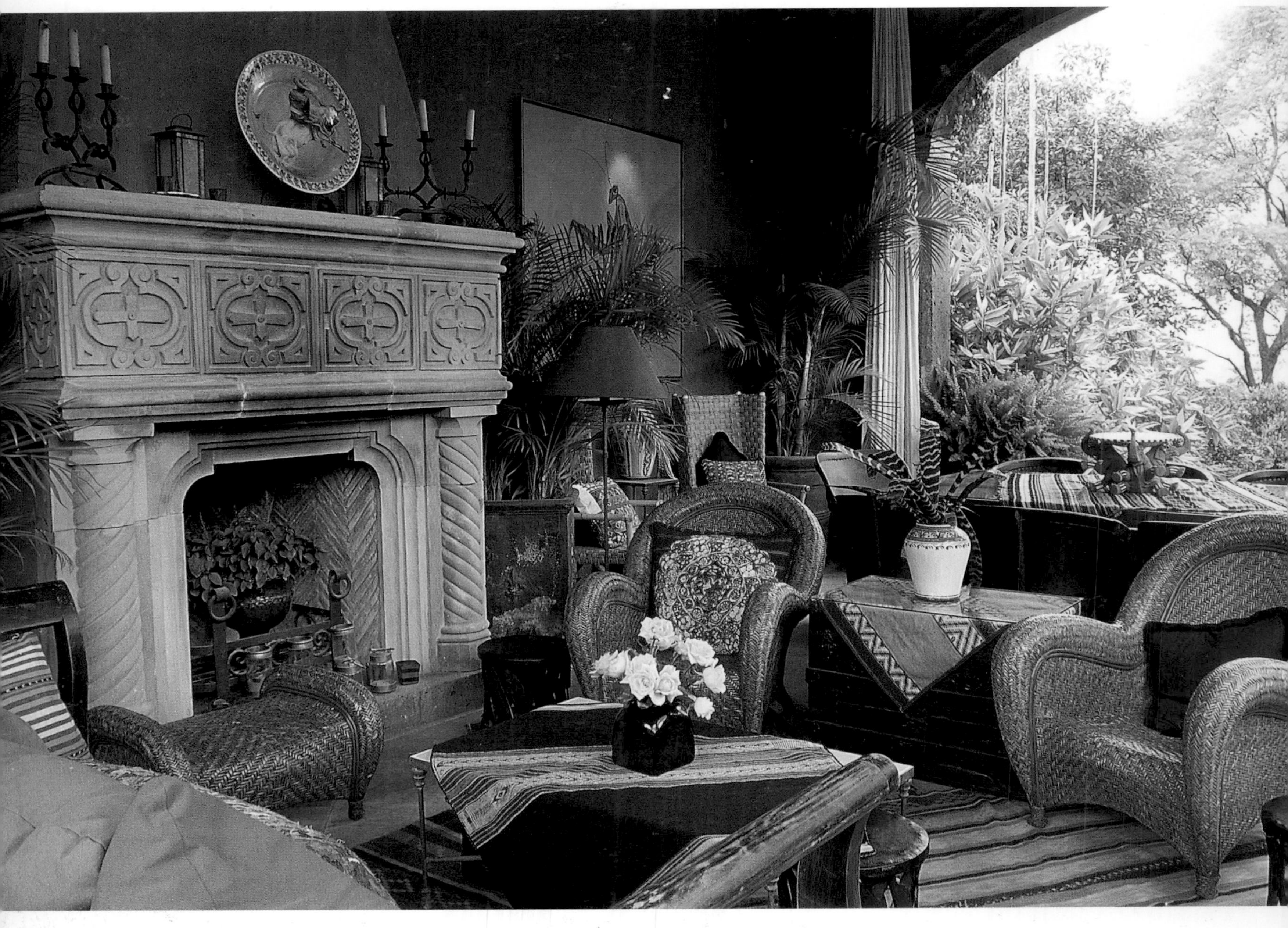

ABOVE: Casa Carolina in San Miguel de Allende features a stand-alone garden living room. The room's centerpiece is a magnificent carved stone fireplace. When the weather is warm, candles and plants fill the hearth rather than roaring fires.

OPPOSITE, TOP: This open space is divided into distinct living and dining areas. The dining table is constructed out of an old door. A thick sheet of glass on top smoothes the table surface while letting the character and texture of the door show through. Sheer white muslin curtains can be drawn across the archway to shield diners' eyes from direct sunlight in the late afternoon. The painting of a praying mantis (a feng shui good luck symbol) is by San Miguel de Allende artist Sergio Maldonado.

OPPOSITE, BOTTOM: The elegant entry to the garden living room is lined with potted Boston ferns. A philodendron tree grows in a raised bed to the left of the stairway and fan palms flourish to the right. Two young ficus trees mark the top step.

OPPOSITE: The open-air living room at Casa Correo in San Miguel de Allende flows through a series of arches to a lovely grotto-like water feature. The ceramics collection includes a shiny green pineapple jar from Michoacán and an assortment of early twentieth-century grain and water-storage vessels from Guerrero. Nayarit Cora Indians used the white deer mask in their initiation rites for young men.

BELOW: The guitar-strumming mermaid is the work of Oaxacan master ceramicist José Garcia Antonio.

BELOW: The patio bar at Hotel Casa Oaxaca is tucked under a staircase. Made of cement, its sinuous curve mirrors that of the arch above. The exposed patches of brick and stone add textural interest, as well as provide ventilation for humidity, which helps maintain the plaster finish.

OPPOSITE: A pre-Columbian Mayan stone carving is inset into this bar at Quinta Los Almendros in Mérida.

chapter
7

PATIO BARS

ABOVE: Rich red walls at Casa Luna Quebrada make the contrasting colors sing. The dove-topped candleholder and the ceramic maiden carrying a basket of bougainvillea on her head hail from Michoacán. The two papier-mâché figures that decorate the top of the hutch are of a type traditionally exploded with firecrackers during Easter celebrations.

RIGHT: *Papel picado* (cut paper) banners and colorful oilcloth tablecloths create a festive atmosphere in the outdoor bar. The rustic shade structure is made of *cariso* (a kind of bamboo). The intricate tin lighting fixtures were fabricated locally in San Miguel de Allende.

ABOVE: Antigua Villa Santa Monica is the former San Miguel de Allende residence of Mexican opera singer Padre José Mohica. The ornately carved and painted patio bar sports fanciful cherubs.

RIGHT: The rooftop bar at Casa Vieja in Mexico City is decorated with a tiled painting copied from Diego Rivera's famous work *Los Alcatraces* (The Calla Lilies).

RIGHT AND BELOW: Architect Luis Bosoms Creixell oversaw the transformation of Yucatecan Hacienda San José in the late 1990s from crumbling former sisal plantation to chic resort. The open-air bar occupies what was the *casa de máquinas* (machine house), the plantation factory where agave leaves were processed into rope fiber in the nineteenth century. The dramatic, uncluttered décor consists of soaring cobalt-blue walls, a polished tile floor, and a few dignified black ceramic pots. The floor-to-ceiling burlap panels provide shade, yet allow for views of the estate.

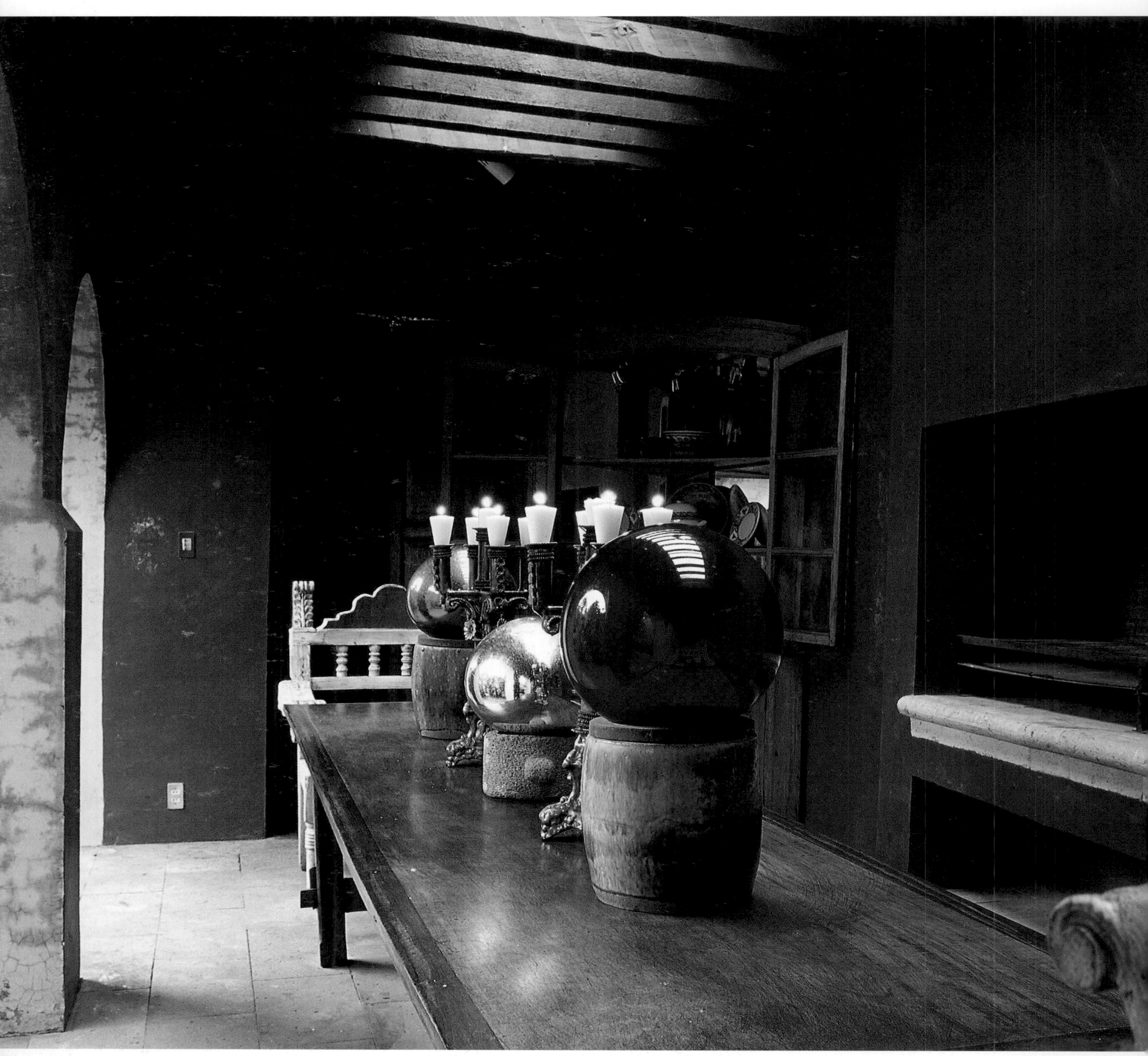

LEFT: At Casa la Roca in Pátzcuaro, the massive scale of the built-in grill complements the open-air dining room's thick Spanish Colonial walls and high ceiling.

BELOW: A carefully placed sago palm bursts like fireworks at the end of this dining corridor at Casa El Deseo near Cuernavaca. The dining table is a relic from a hacienda.

chapter 8

OPEN-AIR DINING ROOMS

OPPOSITE: The narrow dining table at Villa R. is made from recycled oxen yokes and mesquite planks from old houses. The cinnamon-colored chairs were crafted locally in Erongarícuaro.

LEFT: Mirrors in the built-in china hutch allow those diners with their backs to the view to also enjoy the verdant Michoacán landscape.

BELOW: The ceramic pots on either side of the hutch are used for serving *atole* (a porridge-like cornmeal beverage that is often flavored with fruit, such as guavas, strawberries, and plums).

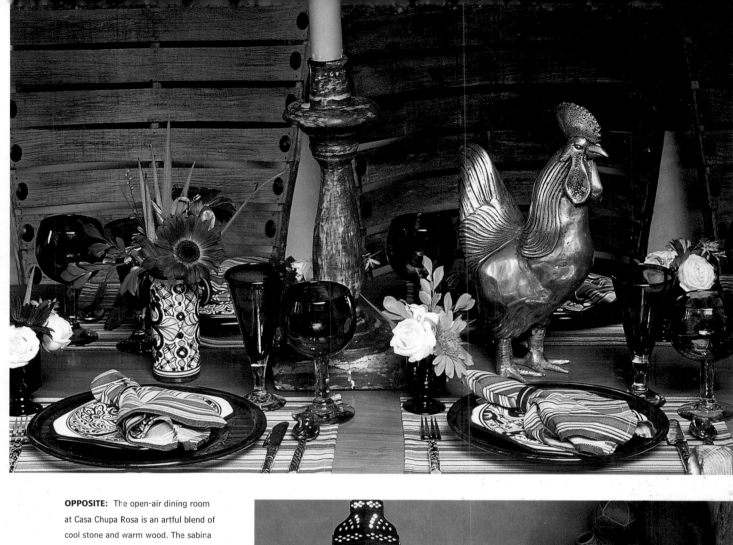

OPPOSITE: The open-air dining room at Casa Chupa Rosa is an artful blend of cool stone and warm wood. The sabina wood table is flanked on one side by rustic high-backed chairs and on the other by a simple bench. Propped against the wall in the back left corner, an antique *piloncillo* (brown sugar cone) mold becomes sculpture. A second one on the sill serves as a candleholder.

ABOVE: The table is set with hand-blown blue glassware and Talavera dishes. The pewter rooster was made in Guadalajara.

RIGHT: Pottery and gourds (traditionally used as water containers) are displayed casually on top of the hutch. Tarahumara Indians carved and painted the curious creature. The net was used for drying and stretching animal skins.

ABOVE: Lunch is served on the terrace at Posada del Tepozteco in Tepoztlán. The trellis overhead is covered with bougainvillea.

TOP: Sculptor Eduardo Olbés made the granite outdoor dining table at Quinta San Gaudencio in Cuernavaca.

MIDDLE: Architect Juan Carlos Valdés describes his design of Casa de Los Cinco Perros in San Miguel de Allende as being "Contemporary Colonial." A barrel-vaulted exposed brick ceiling connects hot pink and purple archways to make this open-air dining room. The modernist geometry of the square wall fountain repeats in the wrought-iron banister.

BOTTOM: Glass gazing balls have been popular in Mexico since the nineteenth century, when they were first imported from Europe. They are both decorative and functional in that they reflect and amplify candlelight. Historically, the globes were placed in dining rooms so that servants could look discreetly into them to see who might need a refill without standing and staring throughout the meal. Gazing balls are also commonly thought to ward off witches, the belief being that witches are so repulsed by the sight of their own reflections that the presence of a gazing ball forces them to flee the premises.

ABOVE: At La Casa de la Real Aduana in Pátzcuaro, a copper pitcher forged in the nearby village of Santa Clara del Cobre holds a bouquet of calla lilies. The indigo-and-white striped bowl is the work of local potter Manuel Morales.

LEFT: Sleepy Shar-Pei dogs lounge on the patio, guarding the hand-carved Mexican dining chairs, each painted a different color, that ring an eighteenth-century farm table.

BELOW: Shocking pink and electric-blue tablecloths contrast with blood-red walls and somber stonework at Casa Luna Quebrada in San Miguel de Allende. Free-spirited color combinations are a hallmark of Mexican design.

OPPOSITE, TOP: Inexpensive dishes from the local *mercado* (market) look cheerful with bright napkins on the Talavera-tiled patio tables at Villa Scorpio Bed and Breakfast in San Miguel de Allende.

OPPOSITE, BOTTOM: Oaxacan chef Pilar Cabrera de Espinoza entertains guests in her patio kitchen at La Casa de los Sabores (House of Flavors). A collection of plates from Puebla decorates the wall.

CHILES MEXICANOS
Mulato
Pasilla Oaxaqueño
Chilhuacle negro
Chilhuacle amarillo
Pasilla Mexicano
Piquin
Morita
Chilpotle

ABOVE: The boundary between outside and inside space blurs at Hacienda San José in the Yucatán, where guests dine under the *portales* (covered porch) or relax with drinks on the stone patio.

OPPOSITE, TOP: Lace tablecloths enhance the mood for fine dining at Maroma Resort. The black tables and chairs are made of cast aluminum. *Palapas* fashioned like wizard hats offer shade on the white sugar beach of the Riviera Maya.

OPPOSITE, BOTTOM: At Las Ranitas (The Little Frogs) in Tulum, coconut palm trees support the terrace shade structure. The name of the house is a sly reference to its French owners.

LEFT: Carved wooden dogs howl at the moon on the ledge above the sink at Casa Chupa Rosa.

BELOW: The outdoor kitchen at Casa Chupa Rosa is decorated with a crazy-quilt pattern of mismatched Talavera tiles on the wall behind the stove.

OPPOSITE, TOP: An ancient laurel tree shelters this outdoor dining area at Hacienda Santa Rosa in the Yucatán.

OPPOSITE, BOTTOM: A patio table set for lunch at Hacienda San Gabriel de las Palmas. Located in the verdant state of Morelos, the hacienda is true to its name in that it is home to some fifteen varieties of palm.

ABOVE: Ever inspired by natural forms, artist Juan Torres uses a conch shell as a water spigot at his home, La Candelaria, in Capula, Michoacán.

LEFT: There is no forgetting that one is in the tropics in the open-air bathroom at Villa Casa Luna in Zihuatanejo.

OPPOSITE: Torres constructed this fantasy bathroom around existing boulders on the property.

chapter

9

GARDEN BATHROOMS

ABOVE: Guests unwind in this smoky blue polished cement tub at Casa Luna Pila Seca in San Miguel de Allende. The surrounding ferns and vines look real by candlelight, but in reality are made of cloth.

RIGHT: The guest bathroom at Casa Areca in San Miguel de Allende has a garden nook built into the marble shower area. A *cantera* stone Madonna sculpture peeks out from a jungle of dracaenas and maidenhair ferns.

FAR RIGHT: An old copper tub has been transformed into a patio sink at La Casa de la Real Aduana in Pátzcuaro.

LEFT: A rain shower pours down into a Jacuzzi at Casa Areca. The house is named for the Areca palms that fill the bathroom. French doors open to a private patio.

LEFT: French doors open to a balcony, letting the sea breeze waft into this dramatic black bathroom at Quinta Maria Cortéz in Puerto Vallarta.

OPPOSITE: An ornately carved courtyard pillar is brought indoors to frame this stone and tile bathtub at Quinta Quebrada in San Miguel de Allende.

BELOW: Two day beds sit side by side on the terrace at Villa R. on Lake Pátzcuaro. The striped orange bedspreads were hand-loomed at nearby Telares Uruapan.

OPPOSITE: A single luxurious fern and a lace-trimmed hammock make for a lovely, quiet corner at Casa El Deseo near Cuernavaca.

chapter 10

BEDS, HAMMOCKS, AND SPAS

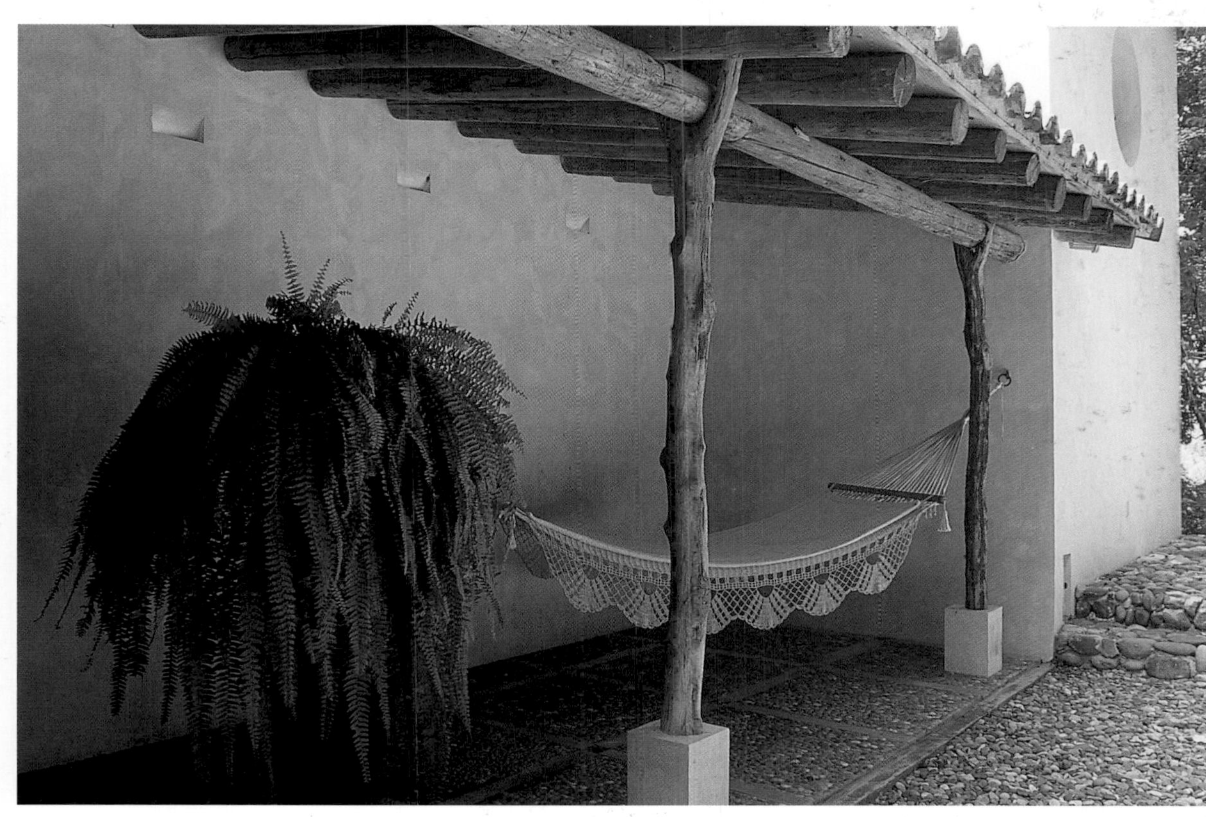

BELOW: At Casa Cerro Sagrado (Sacred Hill House), a retreat center in Teotitlan del Valle, Oaxaca, the porch hammocks are situated to take full advantage of the vista.

OPPOSITE, TOP: Anthropologist Miguel Angel Nuñez's Casa de Tierra (House of Earth) in Erongarícuaro is a traditional Purépecha Indian *troje* (cabin) made of pine planks and carved columns.

OPPOSITE, BOTTOM: The porch looks out on the fertile farmland that abuts Lake Pátzcuaro, where the rainy season each year results in vibrant green foliage.

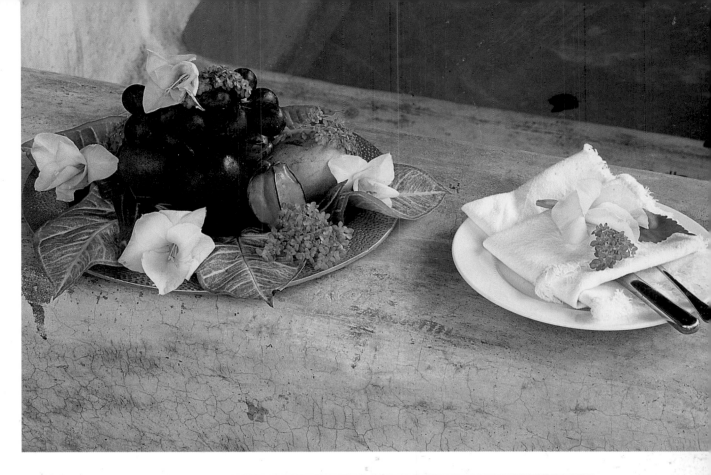

OPPOSITE: Each suite at Hacienda San José in the Yucatán has its own private patio so guests can cool off in their own secluded plunge pools and enjoy long, undisturbed siestas.

TOP: Flowers (in this case hibiscus) and leaves from the garden are artfully arranged to garnish fruit plates, napkins, and the plunge pool itself.

BOTTOM: At Hacienda San José, a sprig of magenta bougainvillea adorns a pair of white towels by the plunge pool. A hedge of elephants ears screens the neighboring patio.

ABOVE: From 1900 to 1920, Hacienda Chichén served as headquarters for the Carnegie Institute's Maya Archeological Expedition. Teams of archeologists lived in cottages that are now hotel guest rooms. Spacious porches with long, sloping roofs are common in the Yucatán, where they provide shelter from sweltering heat and tropical rainstorms.

OPPOSITE, TOP: There are numerous lounging options on this stone terrace at Hacienda Santa Rosa in the Yucatán.

OPPOSITE, BOTTOM: The formal repetition of pillars, beams, and hammocks creates a seductive invitation for a siesta at Hacienda Temozon in the Yucatán.

ABOVE: This hammock floats like a dream above the pool at Hacienda San José in the Yucatán, with shade provided by a rustic pergola.

OPPOSITE, TOP: A massage table for two is situated by the spa *palapa* at El Tamarindo, near Puerto Vallarta.

OPPOSITE, BOTTOM: Guests lounge and enjoy spa treatments on this secluded dock at Paraiso de la Bonita Resort on the Riviera Maya.

chapter

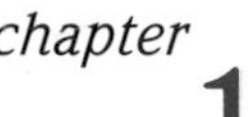

COURTYARD FOUNTAINS

LEFT: The influence of turn-of-the-century French architecture is captured in this peaceful reflecting pool that fills an interior courtyard at Quinta Los Almendros in Mérida. A nineteenth-century French porcelain fountain that depicts three cherubs resting on clouds burbles in the center of the pool.

ABOVE: A beatific Virgin de Soledad presides over this slate fountain at La Casa de la Cuesta in San Miguel de Allende.

OPPOSITE: This courtyard fountain at Casa Luna Quebrada in San Miguel de Allende has a cement surround and base that are colored gray to complement the *cantera* stone wall niche.

RIGHT: Hand-painted Talavera tiles from Dolores Hidalgo line this classic Spanish Colonial fountain at Casa de Sierra Nevada in San Miguel de Allende. Planters and urns add to the blue-and-white theme.

RIGHT: A Moorish-style pine gate opens to a secret garden at Casa Brunson Bed and Breakfast in Pátzcuaro.

OPPOSITE: Owner and architect Timoteo Wachter designed a retractable glass roof to cover this interior courtyard in his home, Casa Areca, in San Miguel de Allende. Plantings around the fish fountain include Swedish ivy, schefflera, and coffee plant.

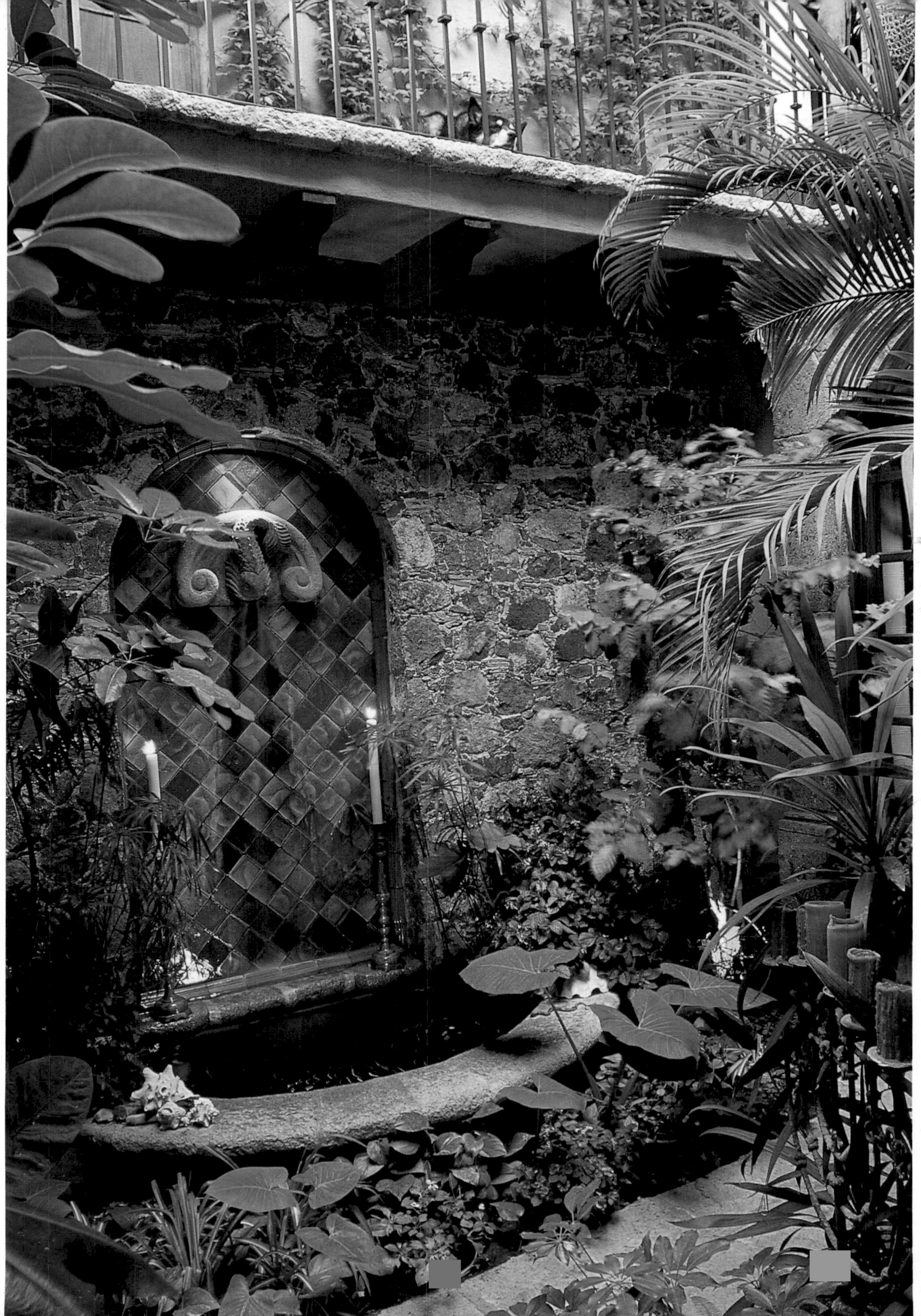

BELOW: Four hundred years ago, nuns washed their robes in this octagonal fountain. Now it serves as a picturesque background for weddings at Hotel Camino Real Oaxaca.

OPPOSITE, LEFT: Lily pads float in this bucolic fountain at Casa Susanna in San Miguel de Allende.

OPPOSITE, RIGHT: Each patio suite at Las Mañanitas in Cuernavaca has its own unique fountain. Stone paving inset with simple tile mosaics shaped like butterflies and flowers surrounds this one. The walls are made of natural adobe bricks.

OPPOSITE AND BELOW: For special occasions such as weddings and birthday parties, courtyard fountains are perfect vessels for extravagant flower arrangements. These are examples of festive fountain bouquets at Posada del Tepozteco in Tepoztlán (opposite) and at Hacienda Cortés in Cuernavaca (below).

ABOVE: Based on a Spanish Colonial design, this *cantera* stone fountain at Casa de Los Cinco Perros in San Miguel de Allende is only eight years old, but looks like it has been around for centuries. Pots of fragrant heliotrope surround the base.

OPPOSITE: The stylized waterfall at Casa Sierra Negra del Sur in San Miguel de Allende is filled with papyrus and iris. Its undulating ledge serves as a gallery for whimsical Ocumicho sculptures. The rusty iron alligator was created in Dolores Hidalgo.

LEFT: Lichen lends a green patina to these steps at Posada del Tepozteco in Tepoztlán.

OPPOSITE, TOP: Carefully manicured creeping fig vines cloak this banister at Casa de la Torre. In Spanish, the plant is called *moneda* because its leaf resembles a coin.

OPPOSITE, BOTTOM: A showy display of impatiens engulfs this wooden bench under the steps.

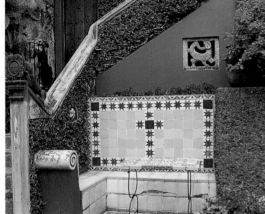

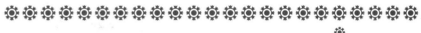

chapter
12

STEPS AND STAIRWAYS

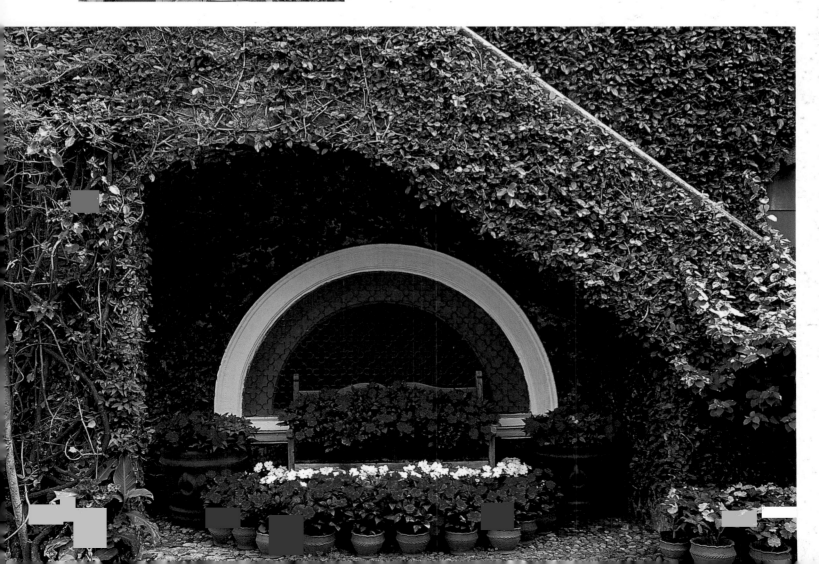

RIGHT: Pots of bright green plume asparagus create a barrier along the edge of this staircase at Casa de Los Cinco Perros in San Miguel de Allende. The striped vase in the foreground is by Oaxacan master potter Dolores Porras.

CENTER: Vivid colors—hot pink, sky blue, avocado green, and golden yellow—splash across these steps at Las Alamandas on the Pacific Coast.

FAR RIGHT: This stairway made of stone, brick, and cement at Casa Chupa Rosa in San Miguel de Allende is an exquisite collage of rough and smooth textures.

ABOVE: A menagerie of locally carved stone sculptures adorns these brick steps at Villa Montaña in Morelia.

OPPOSITE, TOP AND BOTTOM: Villa Montaña's stairways and paths are an eclectic mosaic of black slate, pink *cantera* stone, bricks, and river rocks. Massive stone orbs crown the pillars at the foot of this staircase. Their round shape echoes in the topiary.

LEFT: Furry-looking Japanese grass borders this volcanic basalt stone path at Casa del Alacran (House of the Scorpion) in Tepoztlán. Baby tears grow between the stepping-stones.

ABOVE: Scalloped stone steps lead to the rear courtyard at Casa Susanna in San Miguel de Allende. The neighboring buildings look plenty realistic, but are in fact decorative faux facades.

RIGHT: A lush palette of plants in beds and containers creates a variety of interesting colors and textures along this slate path at Casa de Los Cinco Perros.

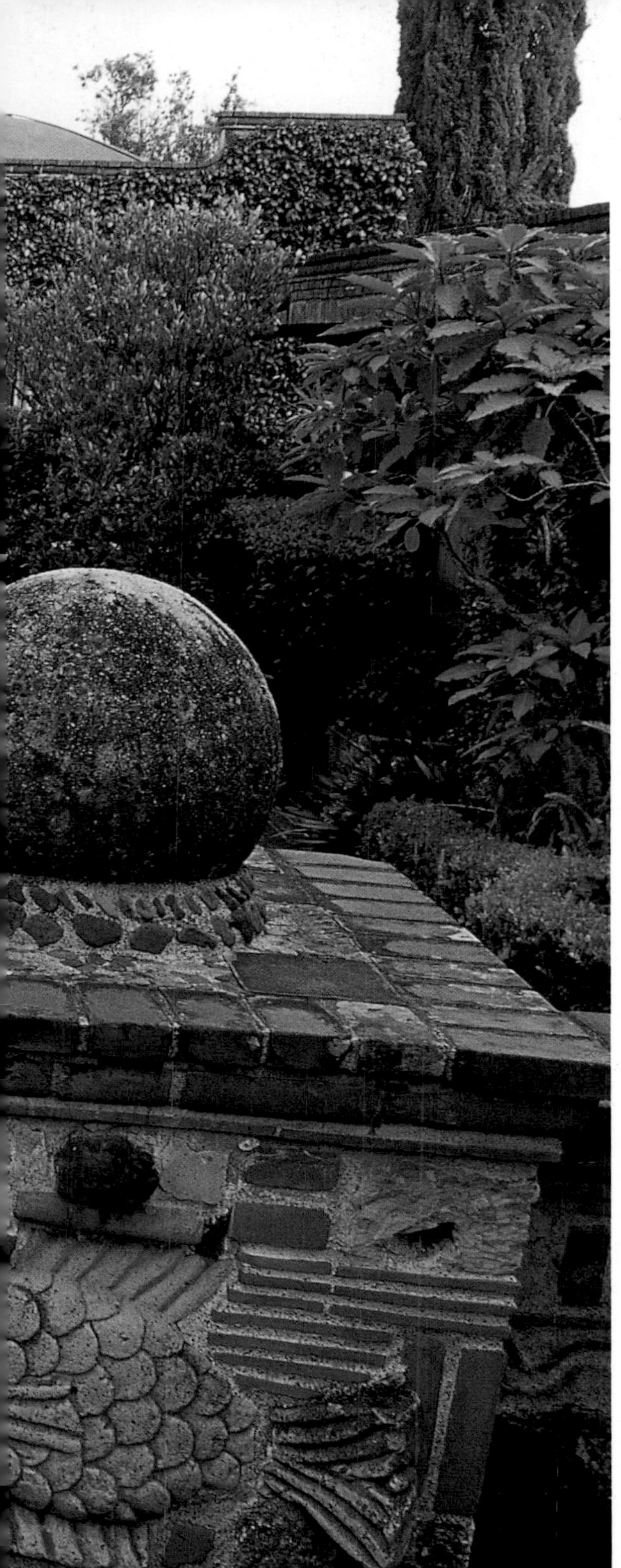

chapter 13

BRICKWORK AND STONEWORK

ABOVE: This slate bench at Casa Ahuilayan in Cuernavaca has a built-in stone backrest. The name of the house means "place of enchantment" in Nahuatl.

LEFT: The masons who created this patio at Villa Montaña in Morelia display stunning creativity.

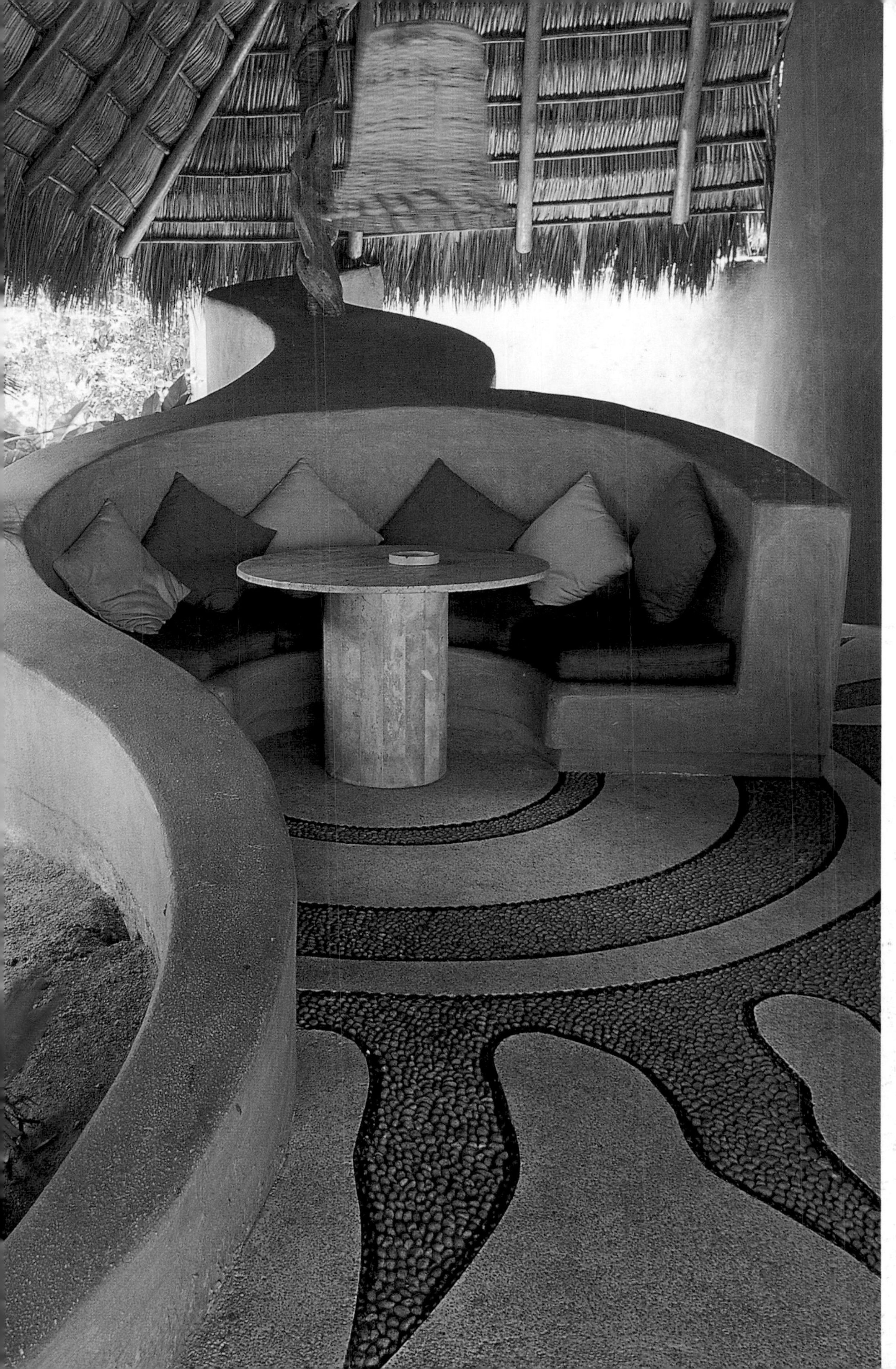

OPPOSITE AND LEFT: Carpets deteriorate quickly in open-air buildings from exposure to the elements. Mexican craftsmen solve this problem by creating stone and concrete floor mosaics that are durable, easy to maintain, and, above all, beautiful. Here are two Pacific Coast examples of floors that feature sun patterns at Las Alamandas (opposite) and El Tamarindo (left).

BELOW: This new construction in the garden at Casa de la Buena Vista (House of the Good View) in San Miguel de Allende looks like an ancient aqueduct. The use of flat brick to form the arches adds an exciting decorative element to the stone structure.

OPPOSITE, TOP: Saint Michael, patron saint of San Miguel de Allende, guards the entrance to La Casa de la Cuesta. The star mosaic paving is made of slate and quartz. The craftsmanship is so fine, the floor is a piece of art.

OPPOSITE, BOTTOM: A mosaic of smooth river stones carpets a corridor at Paraiso de la Bonita Resort on the Riviera Maya. The hand-hewn posts and beams are made from *zapote* tree trunks.

TA ES LA VIDA"

chapter 14

GARDEN SITTING AREAS

OPPOSITE: The images painted on these two chairs at Villa R. are based on nineteenth-century Mexican *costumbrista* folk art paintings that concerned the social customs of the day. The chairs were crafted locally in Erongarícuaro by mfa/eronga inc. The turtle table is *cantera* stone painted with lacquers and enamels.

BELOW: The combination of banana-yellow walls and leafy banana trees gives this patio a distinctly tropical air at Hacienda Chichén Resort in Chichén Itzá.

OPPOSITE, TOP: Families from Mexico City flock to Cuernavaca on weekends to eat, drink, and relax on the lawn at Las Mañanitas.

OPPOSITE, BOTTOM: This thatched-roof *palapa*, outfitted with *equipal* furnishings, is located in the middle of the garden at Casa de Los Cinco Perros in San Miguel de Allende. The fine Talavera centerpiece, a *tibor* (vase), comes from Puebla.

RIGHT: Adirondack chairs painted tropical blue look right at home on the palm-shaded lawn at Villa Capricornio on the Riviera Maya.

BELOW: Maroma Resort architect José Luis Moreno custom-designed these sophisticated mahogany chaise longues for the hotel.

ABOVE: Sculptor Eduardo Olbés made this granite picnic table for his home, Casa del Alacran, in Tepoztlán. The sculptural shapes of succulents and cacti provide the perfect foil for the prehistoric-looking furniture.

LEFT: Sunny days inspire impromptu garden sitting; guests brought these two *equipal* chairs outside from their room at Posada del Tepozteco in Tepoztlán.

OPPOSITE, TOP: This patio furniture in Casa Luna Pila Seca's Starlight Lounge is made of *cariso*, a kind of bamboo that grows in the outskirts of San Miguel de Allende.

OPPOSITE, BOTTOM: These quirky willow furnishings at Casa Luna Pila Seca were constructed in Michoacán.

RIGHT: Fabrica de Luz (Workshop of Light) is the name contemporary artists Ivonne Kennedy and Rubén Leyva gave their home in Oaxaca. On the patio, an old cast-iron stove functions as an outdoor fireplace.

BELOW: The painting studio at Fabrica de Luz opens onto this serene courtyard.

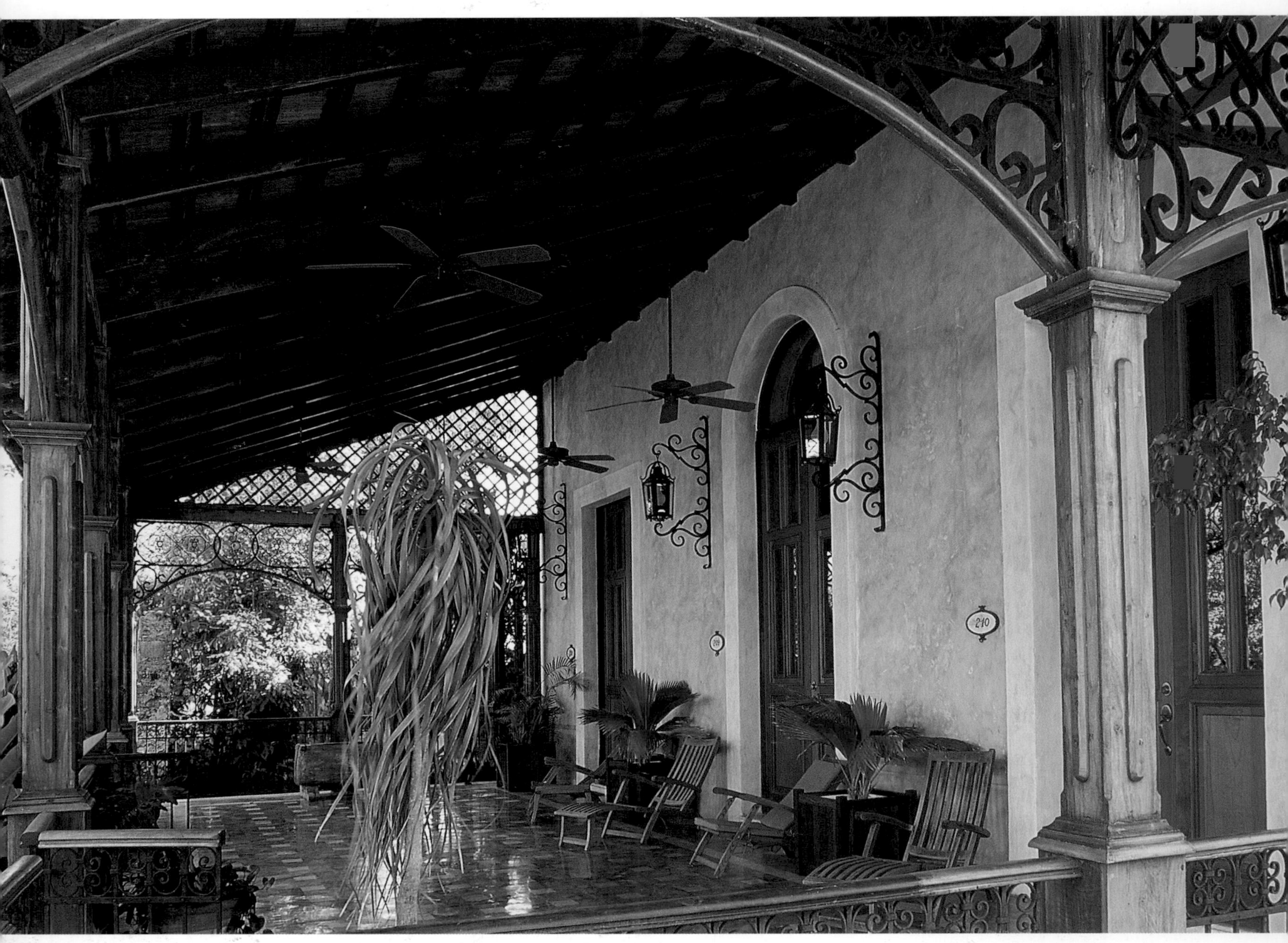

ABOVE: This garden veranda at Hacienda Xcanatún is paved with marble and coral stone quarried locally in the Yucatán. While the botanical name for the hairy plant in the foreground is *Beaucarnea pliabilis*, the gardeners call it *despeinada* (uncombed).

OPPOSITE, TOP: The minimalist plantings at Fabrica de Luz ensure that each plant in the garden—including euphorbia, Easter lily cactus, and ponytail palm—can be appreciated for its sculptural quality.

OPPOSITE, BOTTOM: The homeowners' artwork is exhibited in the loggia. The oil painting at the end of the corridor is by Rubén Leyva and the smaller one is by Ivonne Kennedy.

LEFT: "Maternidad" (Motherhood) by Víctor Manuel Contreras distinguishes the grounds at Las Mañanitas in Cuernavaca.

BELOW AND OPPOSITE: Contemporary bronze statues are by Francisco Zuñiga.

chapter 15

GARDEN SCULPTURE AND STATUARY

OPPOSITE, TOP: The tradition of stone carving in Mexico goes back thousands of years, with subjects ranging from pre-Columbian deities to Christian iconography to all sorts of animals, both realistic and imaginary. Saint Michael emerges from a manicured hedge at the Villa Montaña in Morelia.

OPPOSITE, BOTTOM: Five devout figures pray at a miniature sacred *cenote* (natural waterhole). Hacienda Xcanatún's owner, film director Jorge Ruz Buenfil, commissioned these bronze sculptures based on his drawings. He plans to eventually make life-sized versions of the figures.

RIGHT AND BELOW: The pool garden at Casa Colonial in Cuernavaca is populated by some two dozen *cantera* stone statues, many of which depict saints and other religious icons.

ABOVE AND OPPOSITE TOP: Statues of a happy couple rowing a chicken-shaped boat and of an owl adorn the grounds of Villa Montaña.

OPPOSITE, BOTTOM: These stone animal sculptures at Casa Brunson Bed and Breakfast in Pátzcuaro are from Degollado, a town in Jalisco known for stonework. The ceramic dog figurines on the back step are reproductions of pre-Columbian clay artifacts that were found in tombs in the state of Colima.

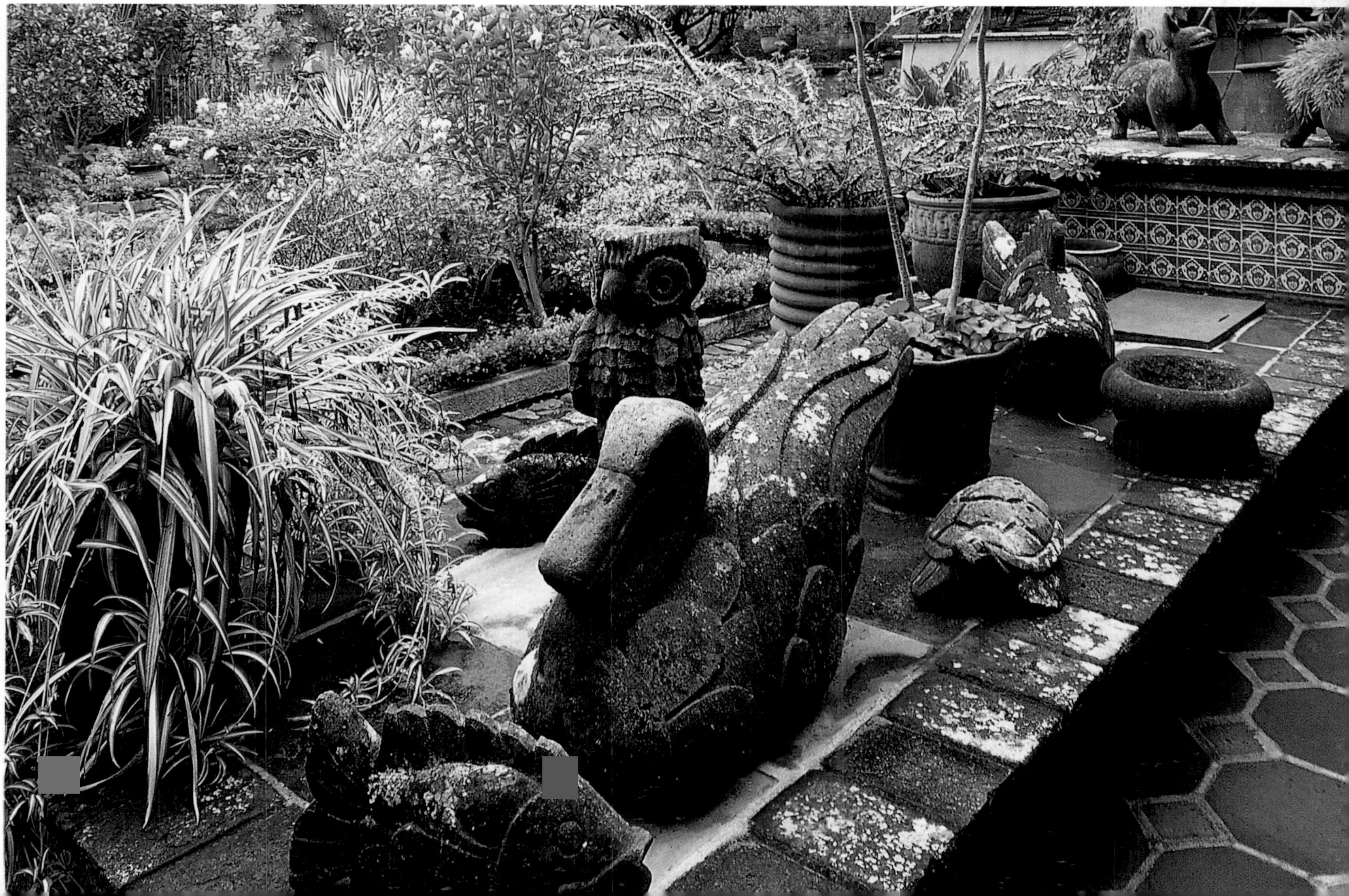

BELOW: A sculpture of the Mayan rain god Chac Mool reclines at Maroma Resort on the Riviera Maya.

OPPOSITE, TOP: Saint Francis of Assisi, the patron saint of animals, tends to a bird at Casa Brunson Bed and Breakfast in Pátzcuaro. The garden features a vibrant blend of succulents as well as native and tropical plants.

BELOW, LEFT: A pre-Columbian Aztec goddess figure peers out from the tropical foliage at Quinta San Gaudencio in Cuernavaca.

BELOW, RIGHT: This stone cross at the Casa de la Torre in Cuernavaca dates back to the Spanish Colonial era in Mexico, when crusading friars preached to the natives outdoors in church courtyards. The cross is carved with symbols that represent the Passion of Christ.

BELOW: The pool garden at Las Mañanitas in Cuernavaca slopes down to a shallow pond where the resident king birds feed.

OPPOSITE: Designer Diane Minter situated the pond in the Las Mañanitas wedding annex around an existing royal palm tree. The pond features a miniature island and two spouting fountains.

chapter 16

GARDEN PONDS

OPPOSITE: A nineteenth-century copper vessel that was originally part of a Puebla distillery functions as a lily pond at Hacienda Xcanatún in the Yucatán. Water lilies are called *naab* in Mayan and are believed to welcome the dawn.

ABOVE: The sinuous pond at Casa Xonulco in Tepoztlán is full of pickerel rush, canna and tiger lilies, Louisiana iris, papyrus, and water hyacinth. The name of the house means "place of peace" in Nahuatl.

RIGHT: This pond and fountain marks the entrance to Maroma Resort on the Riviera Maya. A carved wooden jaguar stalks along the foreground edge while Mayan god Chac Mool watches over from the rear.

BELOW: Avid plant collectors, Therese Kutt and Jack Reinhart converted their swimming pool into an extravagant pond at Casa de Los Cinco Perros in San Miguel de Allende. The pond features more than a dozen different varieties of water lilies, some blooming by day and others by night. The water jet aerates the pond and serves as a stylish fountain.

ABOVE: A waterfall fountain pours into a rocky pond at Casa del Parque (House of the Park) in San Miguel de Allende.

LEFT: Earthenware pots filled with pink geraniums ring this tranquil courtyard pond at Ex-hacienda Molina de Agua (a former mill) near San Miguel de Allende. A thick layer of water hyacinth covers the pond surface.

ABOVE: A water tank, formerly used to irrigate the sisal plantation, was converted into a swimming pool at Hacienda Santa Rosa in the Yucatán. One can swim under the arches into a cool indoor pool area.

LEFT: The pools at Hacienda Temozon in the Yucatán are also transformed cisterns. A water trough flows into this circular wading pool; it is perfectly aligned with the swim-up bar at the far end of the main pool.

chapter 17

SWIMMING POOLS

BELOW: The soft, shimmering blue of the water is a result of light reflecting off the natural sealant used to waterproof the pools. For centuries, the Mayans have used this paste of burned *chukum* tree resin, water, and lime as a sealant. The pool columns at Hacienda Temozon, added as iconic design elements, have gentle bubblers on top that drizzle water down the sides.

ABOVE AND LEFT: The pool at the Oaxaca home of gallery owner Mary Jane Gagnier and master weaver Arnulfo Mendoza is decorated with mosaic sea creatures designed by Mendoza. Tropical plantings that come right to the pool's edge lend an atmosphere of privacy and seclusion.

OPPOSITE, TOP: This pool floor mosaic at Shangri-La Caribe Hotel in Playa del Carmen depicts the Mayan hieroglyphic Hunab-Ku. The ancient symbol is said to inspire spiritual balance and flow.

OPPOSITE, BOTTOM: A cheerful pattern of blue and yellow tiles, two dramatic urns, and a smiling sun decorate this pool at Casa de la Torre in Cuernavaca.

LEFT AND ABOVE: Every welcoming detail—from baskets of plush towels to sprigs of bougainvillea casually placed on prearranged sunbathing mats—has been thought out at Maroma Resort on the Riviera Maya. Coconut, royal, and *xit* palm trees surround the pool.

BELOW: A sensuous infinity pool appears to merge with the ocean at El Tamarindo near Puerto Vallarta.

OPPOSITE, TOP LEFT: The Quinta Quebrada pool in San Miguel de Allende has four underwater loveseats punctuated by horse-shaped stone waterspouts.

OPPOSITE, TOP RIGHT: At Villa Santa Anna in Mérida, Manila palm trees encircle the quatrefoil-shaped swimming pool in the rear courtyard.

OPPOSITE, CENTER LEFT: Bright yellow cushions add zing to the pool terrace furnishings at Casa Colonial in Cuernavaca.

OPPOSITE, CENTER RIGHT: At Hacienda San Gabriel de las Palmas near Cuernavaca, owner Jorge Fenton Sr. designed this lagoon-shaped swimming pool by pacing out its shape while an assistant marked his steps with chalk.

OPPOSITE, BOTTOM LEFT: The Mayan god Zim Na presides over this stone-flanked pool at Maroma Resort. The sea grape plant in the foreground produces fruit that can either be eaten raw, be made into jelly, or be fermented into wine.

OPPOSITE, BOTTOM RIGHT: Bordering the swimming pool at Las Mañanitas in Cuernavaca are giant clay pots overflowing with bougainvillea. Manicured boxwood hedges ring the towering queen palm trees.

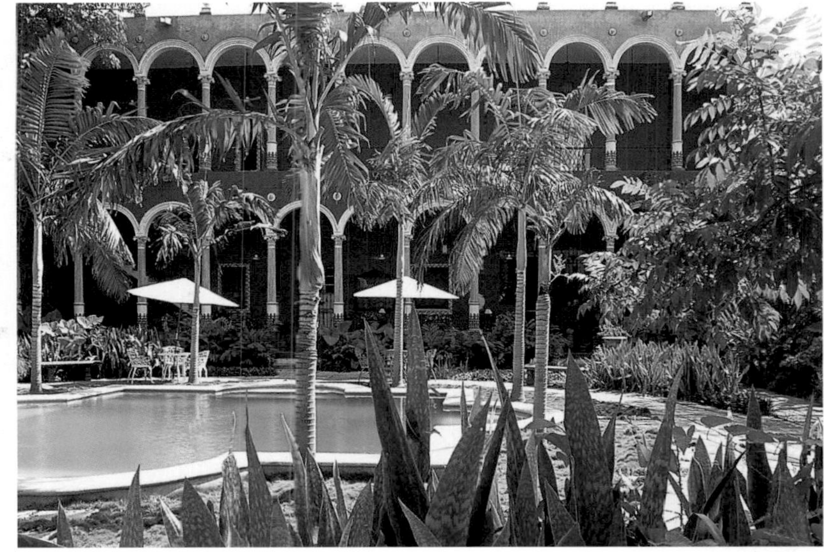

OPPOSITE AND TOP: Clean lines and elegant simplicity define the swimming pools at Casa El Deseo (opposite) near Cuernavaca and at Casa Sol de Oriente (top) in the Casas de Careyes development near Puerto Vallarta.

MIDDLE: At the formal and elegant Casa Susanna in San Miguel de Allende, creeping fig vines blanket the wall behind the swimming pool; white impatiens bloom in the shell-shaped stone wall niche and border the water's edge.

BOTTOM: The interlocking modernist geometry of the swimming pool and hot tub at Casa del Alacran in Tepoztlán includes tiles made of cream-colored travertine and orange-hued limestone.

ABOVE: A charming assortment of ceramic planter sconces adorns this weathered blue patio wall at Villa R. in Erongarícuaro.

GLOSSARY

Cal: Traditional paint pigment made from a mixture of minerals, ground limestone, water, and *nopales* cactus juice

Cantera: Quarry stone used for fountains, statues, doorframes, and fireplaces

Corredor: The corridor is the transition space between courtyard and surrounding rooms. Usually it has arched openings to the courtyard and windows and doors opening to the rooms. This space is also sometimes referred to as the arcade, gallery, or porch. When there are columns rather than arches, it is called a colonnade.

Fuente: Fountain

Hacienda: Large country estate, usually founded as a plantation or for raising cattle

Loggia: A covered space that is open on at least one side to the outdoors; similar to a *corredor*

Mirador: A terrace with a view

Patio: In Mexico, the word *patio* refers to an interior courtyard space enclosed by and closely related to the building, unlike the typical North American patio that faces a garden or lawn.

Sala: Living room

Zaguán: Covered entryway that leads from the street to the courtyard

ABOVE: A simple, striking centerpiece plucked fresh from the garden.

BIBLIOGRAPHY

Aprahamian, Peter. *Mexican Style*. New York: Universe Publishing, a division of Rizzoli International Publications, Inc., 2000.

Becom, Jeffrey. *Maya Color*. New York: Abbeville Press Publishers, 1997.

Clark, Phil. *A Flower Lover's Guide to Mexico*. Mexico City: Minutiae Mexicana, S.A. de C.V., 1972.

Colle, Marie-Pierre. *Paraíso Mexicano*. New York: Clarkson Potter/Publishers, 2002.

Díaz, Bernal. *The Conquest of New Spain*. Translated by J. M. Cohen. London: Penguin Books, 1963.

Haas, Antonio, and Nicolas Sapieha. *Gardens of Mexico*. New York: Rizzoli International Publications, Inc., 1993.

Holmes, Amanda, and Elena Poniatowska. *Mexican Color*. New York: Stewart, Tabori & Chang, 1998.

Kirby, Rosina Greene. *Mexican Landscape Architecture*. Tucson, Arizona: The University of Arizona Press, 1972.

McMenamin, Donna. *Traditional Mexican Style Exteriors*. Atglen, Pennsylvania: Schiffer Publishing Ltd., 2003.

Miller, Mary, and Karl Taude. *An Illustrated Dictionary of the Gods and Symbols of Ancient Mexico and the Maya*. London: Thames & Hudson Ltd., 1997.

O'Gorman, Patricia W. *Patios and Gardens of Mexico*. Stamford, Connecticut: Architectural Book Publishing Co. Inc., 1979.

Presman, M. Walter. *Meet Flora Mexicana*. Globe, Arizona: Dale Stuart King, Publisher, 1962.

Reynolds, John S. *Courtyards*. New York: John Wiley & Sons, Inc., 2002.

Rohwer, Jens G. *Tropical Plants of the World*. New York: Sterling Publishing Co., Inc., 2002.

Sayer, Chloe. *The Arts and Crafts of Mexico*. San Francisco: Chronicle Books, 1990.

Schlesinger, Victoria. *Animals & Plants of the Ancient Maya*. Austin, Texas: University of Texas Press, 2001.

Street-Porter, Tim. *Casa Mexicana*. New York: Stewart, Tabori & Chang, 1989.

Villela, Khristaan, Ellen Bradbury, and Logan Wagner. *Contemporary Mexican Design and Architecture*. Layton, Utah: Gibbs Smith, Publisher, 2002.

Wasserspring, Lois, and Vicki Ragan. *Oaxacan Ceramics*. San Francisco: Chronicle Books, 2000.

Witynski, Karen, and Joe P. Carr. *Casa Yucatán*. Layton, Utah: Gibbs Smith, Publisher, 2002.

Witynski, Karen, and Joe P. Carr. *The New Hacienda*. Layton, Utah: Gibbs Smith, Publisher, 1999.

Yampolsky, Mariana, and Chloe Sayer. *The Traditional Architecture of Mexico*. London: Thames and Hudson, Ltd., 1993.

Ypma, Herbert. *Mexican Contemporary*. New York: Stewart, Tabori & Chang, 1997.

Many of the properties featured in this book are now open to the public as inns and resorts. To call Mexico from the United States, dial 011 and then the country code 52 for the following numbers.

Las Alamandas
Apartado Postal 201
San Patricio Melaque, Jalisco 48980
Tel: 322/285-5500
Fax: 322/285-5027
Email: info@alamandas.com
Web: www.alamandas.com

Antigua Villa Santa Monica
Baeza No. 22
San Miguel de Allende, Guanajuato 37700
Tel: 415/152-0427
Fax: 415/152-0518
Email:
antiguavillasantamonica@prodigy.net.mx
Web: www.mexonline.com/smonica.htm

Casa Brunson Bed and Breakfast
Dr. Coss No. 13, Col. Centro
Pátzcuaro, Michoacán 61600
Tel/Fax: 434/342-3903
Email: phyllis@ml.com.mx
Web: www.mexonline.com/casabrunson.htm

Casa Colonial
Netzaualcoyotl No. 37, Col. Centro
Cuernavaca, Morelos 62000
Tel: 777/312-7033
Fax: 777/310-0395
Email: hotelcasaSpanishColonial@hotmail.com
Web: www.tourbymexico.com/casacolo.htm

La Casa Encantada
Dr. Coss No. 15, Col. Centro
Pátzcuaro, Michoacán 61600
Tel: 434/342-3492
Email: encantada@ml.com.mx
Web: www.lacasaencantada.com

Casa Luna Pila Seca and Casa Luna Quebrada
Pila Seca No. 11
San Miguel de Allende, Guanajuato 37700
Tel/Fax: 415/152-1117
Email: casaluna@unisono.net.mx
Web: www.casaluna.com

La Casa de la Cuesta
Cuesta de San José No. 32
San Miguel de Allende, Guanajuato 37700
Tel/Fax: 415/154-4324
Email: info@casadelacuesta.com
Web: www.casadelacuesta.com

La Casa de los Sabores
(Las Bugambilias 2 B&B)
Libres No. 205, Col. Centro
Oaxaca, Oaxaca 68000
Tel: 951/516-5704
Tel/Fax: 951/516-1165
Email: bugambilias@lasbugambilias.com
Web: www.lasbugambilias.com

Casa de Sierra Nevada Quinta Real
Hospicio 35
San Miguel de Allende, Guanajuato 37700
Tel: 415/152-7040
Fax: 415/152-1436
Email: mail@casadesierranevada.com
Web: www.casadesierranevada.com

Casa Vieja
Eugenio Sue 45
Colonia Polanco
Mexico City, Distrito Federal 11560
Tel: 555/282-0067
Fax: 555/281-3780
Email: casaviej@mail.internet.com.mx
Web: www.casavieja.com

Casas de Careyes
Km. 53.5 Carretera Barra de Navidad-Puerto Vallarta
Melaque, Jalisco 48980
Tel: 315/351-0240
Fax: 315/351-0246
Email: info@careyes.com.mx
Web: www.careyes.com.mx

Hacienda Chichén Resort
Carretera Mérida Km. 120
Chichén Itzá, Yucatán 97000
Tel: 999/924-2150
Fax: 999/924-5011
Email: balamhtl@finred.com.mx
Web: www.Yucatanadventure.com.mx

Hacienda San Gabriel de las Palmas
Carretera Federal Cuernavaca-Chilpancingo Km. 41.8
Amacuzac, Morelos 62640
Tel: 751/348-0636
Tel/Fax: 751/348-0113
Email: sangabriel@prodigy.net.mx
Web: www.hacienda-sangabriel.com.mx

Hacienda San José
Carretera Tixkokob-Tekanto Km. 30
Tixkokob, Yucatán 97470
Tel: 999/910-4617
Fax: 999/923-7963
Email: reservations1@grupoplan.com
Web: www.luxurycollection.com

Hacienda Santa Rosa
Carretera Mérida-Champeche Km. 129
Santa Rosa, Yucatán 97800
Tel: 999/910-4875
Fax: 999/923-7963
Email: reservations1@grupoplan.com
Web: www.luxurycollection.com

HOTEL RESOURCE GUIDE

Hacienda Temozon
Carretera Mérida-Uxmal Km. 182
Temozon Sur, Yucatán 97825
Tel: 999/923-8089
Fax: 999/923-7963
Email: reservations1@grupoplan.com
Web: www.luxurycollection.com

Hacienda Xcanatún
Tablaje Rústico Catastral No. 13667
Xcanatún, Yucatán 97300
Tel: 999/941-0273
Fax: 999/941-0213
Email: hacienda@xcanatun.com
Web: www.xcanatun.com

Hotel Camino Real Oaxaca
Cinco de Mayo No. 300
Oaxaca, Oaxaca 68000
Tel: 951/501-6100
Fax: 951/516-0732
E-mail: oax@caminoreal.com
Web: www.caminoreal.com

Hotel Casa Oaxaca
García Vigil No. 407, Col. Centro
Oaxaca, Oaxaca 68000
Tel: 951/514-4173
Fax: 951/516-4412
Email: casaoax@prodigy.net.mx
Web: www.casaoaxaca.com

Las Mañanitas
Ricardo Linares No. 107
Cuernavaca, Morelos 62000
Tel: 777/314-1466
Fax: 777/318-3672
Email: reservaciones@lasmananitas.com.mx
Web: www.lasmananitas.com.mx

Maroma Resort & Spa
Carretera Cancún Tulum Km. 51, Riviera Maya
Solidaridad, Quintana Roo 77710
Tel: 998/ 872-8200
Fax: 998/872-8219
Email: reservations@maromahotel.com
Web: www.maromahotel.com

Paraiso de la Bonita Resort & Thalasso
Carretera Cancun-Chetumal Km. 328, Bahia Petenpich
Cancun, Quintana Roo 77500
Tel: 998/872-8300
Fax: 998/872-8301
Email: resa@paraisodelabonitaresort.com
Web: www.paraiso-bonita.intercontinental.com

Posada del Tepozteco
Paraiso No. 3, Barrio de San Miguel
Tepoztlán, Morelos 62520
Tel: 739/395-0010
Fax: 739/395-0323
Email: tepozhot@prodigy.net.mx
Web: www.tourbymexico.com/posadadel-tepozteco

Quinta Maria Cortéz
126 Calle Sagitario
Playa Conchas Chinas
Puerto Vallarta, Jalisco 48300
Tel: 322/221-5317
Fax: 322/221-5327
Email: info@villasinvallarta.com
Web: www.quinta-maria.com

Rancho Santiago
Rancho Santiago Tzipijo
Between Ihuatzio and Cucuchucho
Pátzcuaro, Michoacán 61600
Tel: 434/344-0880
Email: tzipijo@ml.com.mx
Web: www.geocities.com/theothermexico

Las Ranitas
Carretera Tulum-Boca Paila Km. 9
Tulum, Quintana Roo 77780
Tel/Fax: 984/877-8554
Email: info@lasRanitas.com
Web: www.lasRanitas.com

Shangri-La Caribe Hotel
Calle 38 Norte
Entre 5a Avenida-Zona Federal Maritima
Playa del Carmen, Quintana Roo 77710
Tel: 984/873-0611
Fax: 984/873-0500
Email: info@shangrilacaribe.net
Web: www.shangrilacaribe.net

El Tamarindo
Carretera Melaque-Puerto Vallarta Km 7.5
Cihuatlan, Jalisco 48970
Tel: 315/351-5032
Fax: 315/351-5070
Email: tamarindo@tamarindohotel.com
Web: www.luxurycollection.com

Villa Montana
Patzimba No. 201, Col. Vista Bella
Morelia, Michoacán 58090
Tel: 443/314-0231
Fax: 443/315-1423
Email: hotel@villamontana.com.mx
Web: www.villamontana.com.mx

Villa Scorpio Bed and Breakfast
Quebrada No. 93, Col. Centro
San Miguel de Allende, Guanajuato 37700
Tel: 415/152-7575
Email: villascorpio@unforgettable.com
Web: www.villascorpio.com

We wish to express our gratitude to AeroMexico, Mexicana Airlines, and Sectur, without whose generous support this book would not have been possible. Jorge Gamboa of the Mexican Tourist Office in Los Angeles, Leticia Navarro Ochoa of Sectur, Margie Gostyla and Magdalena Montenegro of AeroMexico, Virginia Borgla of Mexicana Airlines, and Ana Argaiz, Ema Bolio Montero, and Carolina Cardenas of the Morelia Department of Tourism were ever so helpful coordinating the logistics of our travels. Needless to say, we are grateful to all of the homeowners and hotel owners and managers who welcomed us into their enchanted gardens. Their marvelous creativity and hospitality made our work a delight. Heartfelt thanks to Robb Anderson and Ana Isabel Garcia of Reposado, Patricia Edelen of Casa Ahuilayan, Karla Estrada and Bruno Mercenari, Rodrigo Estrada, Juan Fenton of Hacienda San Gabriel de las Palmas, Eduardo Gallo of Las Mañanitas, José Antonio Gonzalez and Roberto Laredo of Casa El Deseo, Rodrigo Guerra of Hotel Hosteria Las Quintas Eco Spa, Ana and Juan Pons of Casa Colonial and Restaurante Casa Hidalgo, Nadine Vinot-Postry of Casa Leof, Gabriela Rodriguez Vizcarra, Sally Sloan of the Robert Brady Museum, and Elia and Rodolpo Stavenhagen of Quinta San Gaudencio all in the Cuernavaca, Morelos area; to Gabriela and Pablo Barbachano of Quinta Los Almendros, Isabel Barbachano-Gordon of Hacienda Chichén Resort and Hotel Casa del Balam, Cristina Baker, Jorge Ruz Buenfil, and Nicolas Wright of Hacienda Xcanatún, Herman Reeling Brouwer and Daniel Mellado of Hacienda Temozon, Karsten Lemke of Hacienda Santa Rosa, Anthony Stanford of Villa Santa Anna, Veronique Timsonet of Hacienda San José, and Luis de Yturbe all in the Mérida, Yucatán region; to Eva, Nicolas, and Philippe de Reiset of Villa Montaña in Morelia, Michoacán; to Mauricio Barragan and Luis Sosa of Casa Vieja, Luis Bosoms Creixell of Grupo Plan, and Patricia Ortiz of Four Seasons Mexico City in Mexico City, Distrito Federal; to Maria Angeles Juncadella, Noel Cayetano Castro, and Diego Gonzalez of Galería Indigo, Mercede Audelo and Jorge Quintanar Castillo, Rosa Blum and Henry Wangeman of Amate Bookstore, Aurora Cabrera, Don Dawson, and Alvaro Rocha of Las Bugambilias B&B, Pilar Cabrera de Espinoza and Luis Espinoza of La Casa de los Sabores and La Olla Café-Galería, Rene Cabrera and Adriana Zavala Quiroz of La Casa de los Milagros B&B, Alexandre de Brouwer of Hotel Camino Real Oaxaca, Mary Jane Gagnier and Arnulfo Mendoza of Galería La Mano Magica and Casa Cerro Sagrado, Peter Handel, Ivonne Kennedy and Rubén Leyva of Fabrica de Luz, Fernando Martín del Campo of Hotel Victoria, Jane and Thorny Robison of Casa Colonial, Alejandro Ruiz and Gabriela Salinas of Hotel Casa Oaxaca, and Gary Titus all in Oaxaca, Oaxaca; to Miguel Angel Nuñez of Casa de Tierra, Didier Dorval and Gemma Macouzet of La Casa de la Real Aduana, Arminda Flores and Kevin Quigley of Rancho Santiago, Edward Holler and Samuel Saunders of Casa la Roca, Deborah Peacock, Maureen and Steve Rosenthal of Villa R., Victoria

ACKNOWLEDGMENTS

Ryan of La Casa Encantada, Jon and Phyllis Skaglund of Casa Brunson B&B, Meg Snyder, and Belia and Juan Torres of La Candelaria all in the Pátzcuaro, Michoacán region; to "Silver" Alexander and Margaret Parrish of Quinta Maria Cortéz, Gian Franco Brignone and Giorgio Brignone of Casas de Careyes, Isabel Goldsmith of Las Alamandas, and Ji Hyun Park of El Tamarindo all in the Puerto Vallarta, Jalisco area; to José Antonio Bugarín, Carlos Gosselin, and Abbey Nayer of Paraiso de la Bonita Resort & Thalasso, Ramón Carlos Aguayo, Felipe Espinoza, José Luis Moreno, Sally Shaw Moreno, and Hugo Oliva of Maroma Resort & Spa, Clint E. Ball and William Lubcke of Shangri-La Caribe Hotel, Dos Ceibas, and Yannik Piel and Leila Voight of Las Ranitas all in the Riviera Maya, Quintana Roo region; to Sudhir Amembal and Kiran Puri of Casa del Parque, Bill and Pepe Anderson of Casa de la Buena Vista, Evita Avery of La Calaca Arte Popular, Bill Begalke and Rodd Rodriguez, Susan Bloom of Casa Susanna, Marsha Brown of Ex-hacienda Molina de Agua, Alex Caragonne and Margie Shackelford of Casa Correo, Betty and Nick Coates of Casa Seis Fuentes, Caren and David Cross, Beverly Donofrio, Richard Dupuis of Allende Properties, Esa Everroad, Ann and Butch Futch and Cynthia Whitney-Ward of Casa Chupa Rosa, Penelope Haskew and Nicholas Power of Villa Scorpio B&B, Cathi and Steven House of Casa Beso de las Estrellas, Leigh Hyams of Casa Sierra Negra del Sur, Martha Hyder of Quinta Quebrada, Dianne Kushner of Casa Luna Pila Seca and Casa Luna Quebrada, Norm and Pat Lacayo, Carol and Robert Latta of Casa Carolina, Bill and Heidi LeVasseur of La Casa de la Cuesta, Charles and Mary Marsh of Casa Fresno Grande, Susan McKinney de Ortega, Anado McLauchlin, Susan Plum, Therese Kutt and Jack Reinhart of Casa de Los Cinco Perros, Zoe Siegel, Malena Skåtun and Timoteo Wachter of Casa Areca, Betse Strang, Harold and Jamie Stream, Elsa and Merle Wachter, Theresa Wachter, and Patrice Wynne all in San Miguel de Allende, Guanajuato; to Mílada Bazant, Alejandro Camerena of Posada del Tepozteco, Patricia Hogan, Dr. Ignacio and Maria Maldonado of Casa Xonulco, Diane Mitner of Habitat Jardínes Acuáticos, Eduardo Olbés of Casa del Alacran, and Anita and Bill Smith all in the Tepoztlán, Morelos area; to Patsy and Joe LoGiudice of Villa Casa Luna in Zihuatanejo; and to those homeowners who wish to remain anonymous. ❁ We are grateful as ever to our fabulous agents, Sarah Jane Freyman and Amy Rennert, to A&I Color Lab in Santa Monica, and to Fuji Film for their consistently excellent work. And for their personal support on this project, *abrazos* to Dave and Annalena Barrett, Hugh Levick, Anne Burt, and Susan Davis. Lastly, at Chronicle Books, we thank editors Lisa Campbell and Leslie Jonath, copy editor Carolyn Keating, art director Vanessa Dina, designer Deborah Bowman, production coordinator Steve Kim, Jan Hughes, Doug Ogan, Nion McEvoy, and the rest of the swell gang. They are all just the greatest.

—M.L. and G.H.

ABOVE: Homeowner Arminda Flores cooks Purépecha specialties in her rustic open-air kitchen at Rancho Santiago near Pátzcuaro.

All reasonable effort has been made to trace the holders of copyright. Any om or errors are inadvertent and will be corrected in subsequent editions, provid notification is sent to the publisher. Grateful acknowledgment is made for per sion to reprint quotes from the following sources:

Page 9 from *Fifteen Poets of the Aztec World* by Miguel León-Portilla. © 1992 Miguel León-Portilla. Used with permission of University of Oklahoma Press.

Page 11 "The South" by Jorge Luis Borges, translated by W. S. Merwin, copyr © 1999 by Maria Kodama; translation copyright © 1999 by W. S. Merwin, fr *Selected Poems* by Jorge Borges, edited by Alexander Coleman. Used with pe sion of Viking Penguin, a division of Penguin Group (USA) Inc.